Integrated Chinese

中文听说读写

Simplified Character Edition
Workbook

Tao-chung Yao and Yuehua Liu
Yea-fen Chen, Liangyan Ge and Xiaojun Wang

Cheng & Tsui Company

First edition 1997
2002 printing

Cheng & Tsui Company
25 West Street
Boston, MA 02111-1213 USA

Simplified Character Edition
ISBN 0-88727-271-1

Companion textbooks, character workbooks and audio tapes are also available from the publisher.

Printed in the United States of America

PREFACE

In designing *Integrated Chinese, Level One* workbook exercises, we strove to give equal emphasis to the students' listening, speaking, reading, and writing skills. There are different difficulty levels in order to provide variety and flexibility to suit different curriculum needs. Teachers should assign the exercises at their discretion; they should not feel pressured into using all of them and should feel free to use them out of sequence, if appropriate. Moreover, teachers can complement this workbook with their own exercises.

I. Listening Comprehension

All too often listening comprehension is sacrificed in a formal classroom setting because of time constraint. Students tend to focus their time and energies on the mastery of a few grammar points. This workbook tries to remedy this imbalance by including a substantial number of listening comprehension exercises.

There are two categories of listening exercises; both can be done on the students' own time or in the classroom. In either case, it is important to have the instructor review the students' answers for accuracy.

The first category of listening exercises consists of a tape recording of each lesson. For the exercises to be meaningful, students should *first* study the vocabulary list, *then* listen to the recordings *before* attempting to read the texts. The questions are provided to help students' aural understanding of the texts and to test their reading comprehension.

The second category of listening exercises consists of a tape recording of three or more mini-dialogues or solo narrations. These exercises are designed to recycle the vocabulary and grammar points introduced in the new lesson. Some of the exercises are significantly more difficult since students are asked to choose among several possible answers. These exercises, therefore, should be assigned towards the end of a lesson, when the students have become more familiar with the contents of the texts.

II. Speaking Exercises

Here, too, there are two types of exercises. However, they are designed for different levels of proficiency within each lesson and should be assigned at the appropriate time. In the first type, to help students apply their newly-acquired vocabulary and grammatical understanding to meaningful communication, we ask concrete, personal questions related to their daily lives. These questions require a one or two-sentence answer. By stringing together short questions and answers, students can construct their own mini-dialogues, practice in pairs or take turns asking or answering the questions.

Once they have gained confidence, students can progress to more difficult questions where they are invited to express opinions on a number of topics. Typically, these questions are abstract, so the students will gradually learn to express their opinions and give their answers in paragraph-length discourse. As the school year progresses, these types of questions should take up more class discussion time. Because this second type of speaking exercise is quite challenging, it should be attempted only *after* students are well-grounded in the grammar and vocabulary of a particular lesson. This is usually *not immediately* after completing the first part of the speaking exercises.

III. Reading Comprehension

There are three to four passages for reading comprehension in each lesson. The first passage--usually short and related to the lesson at hand--recycles vocabulary and grammar points.

The second passage consists of slightly modified authentic materials, such as print advertisements, announcements, school diplomas, newspaper articles, etc. This passage may contain some unfamiliar vocabulary. The purpose of these materials is to train students to scan for useful information and not to let the appearance of a few new words distract them from comprehending the "big picture." Here, the teacher has a particularly important role to play in easing the students' anxiety about unfamiliar vocabulary. Teachers should encourage the student to ask: What do I really need to look for in a job announcement, a personal ad, or movie listings? Students should refer frequently to the questions to help them decipher these materials and should resist looking up every new word in their dictionary.

IV. Writing and Grammar Exercises

A. Grammar and Usage

These drills and exercises are designed to solidify the students' grasp of important grammar points. Through brief exchanges, students answer questions using specific grammatical forms or are given sentences to complete. By providing context for their exercises, students gain a clearer understanding of the grammar points and will not treat them as simple, mechanical repetition drills.

Towards the last quarter of the lessons, students are introduced to increasingly sophisticated and abstract vocabulary. Corresponding exercises help them to grasp the nuances of new words. For example, synonyms are a source of great difficulty, so exercises are provided to help students distinguish between them.

B. Translation

Translation has been a tool for language teaching throughout the ages, and positive student feedback confirms our belief that it continues to play an important role. The exercises we have devised serve to reinforce two primary areas: one, to get students to apply specific grammatical structures; two, to allow students to build on their ever-increasing vocabulary. Ultimately, our hope is that this dual-pronged approach will enable students to understand that it takes more than just literal translation to convey an idea in a foreign language.

C. Composition

This is the culmination of the written exercises and is where students learn to express themselves in writing. Many of the topics overlap with those used in oral practice. We expect that students will find it easier to put in writing what they have already learned to express orally.

TABLE OF CONTENTS

Preface..i

Table of Contents...iii

Lesson Twelve: **Dining**...................................1
   I. Listening Comprehension................................1
   II. Speaking Exercises.......................................2
   III. Reading Comprehension...............................3
   IV. Writing and Grammar Exercises....................6

Lesson Thirteen: **At the Library**....................13
   I. Listening Comprehension..............................13
   II. Speaking Exercises.....................................14
   III. Reading Comprehension.............................15
   IV. Writing and Grammar Exercises..................18

Lesson Fourteen: **Asking Directions**.............23
   I. Listening Comprehension..............................23
   II. Speaking Exercises.....................................24
   III. Reading Comprehension.............................25
   IV. Writing and Grammar Exercises..................29

Lesson Fifteen: **Birthday Party**.....................39
   I. Listening Comprehension..............................39
   II. Speaking Exercises.....................................40
   III. Reading Comprehension.............................42
   IV. Writing and Grammar Exercises..................45

Lesson Sixteen: **Seeing a Doctor**..................53
   I. Listening Comprehension..............................53
   II. Speaking Exercises.....................................54
   III. Reading Comprehension.............................56
   IV. Writing and Grammar Exercises..................59

Lesson Seventeen: **Dating**.............................65
   I. Listening Comprehension..............................65
   II. Speaking Exercises.....................................66

III. Reading Comprehension...67
IV. Writing and Grammar Exercises..69

Lesson Eighteen: **Renting an Apartment**...............................75
I. Listening Comprehension..75
II. Speaking Exercises...76
III. Reading Comprehension..77
IV. Writing and Grammar Exercises..79

Lesson Nineteen: **Post Office**..83
I. Listening Comprehension..83
II. Speaking Exercises...84
III. Reading Comprehension..85
IV. Writing and Grammar Exercises..87

Lesson Twenty: **Sports**...93
I. Listening Comprehension..93
II. Speaking Exercises...94
III. Reading Comprehension..95
IV. Writing and Grammar Exercises..97

Lesson Twenty-One: **Travel**..103
I. Listening Comprehension...103
II. Speaking Exercises..104
III. Reading Comprehension...105
IV. Writing and Grammar Exercises...108

Lesson Twenty-Two: **Hometown**...117
I. Listening Comprehension...117
II. Speaking Exercises..118
III. Reading Comprehension...119
IV. Writing and Grammar Exercises...122

Lesson Twenty-Three: **At the Airport**...................................129
I. Listening Comprehension...129
II. Speaking Exercises..131
III. Reading Comprehension...132
IV. Writing and Grammar Exercises...135

Lesson Twelve   Dining

I. Listening Comprehension

Section One (Listen to the tape for the textbook) (True/False)

A. Dialogue I
(   ) 1. There are no seats left in the restaurant.
(   ) 2. The woman doesn't eat meat, but the man does.
(   ) 3. They both ordered hot and sour soup.
(   ) 4. They both ordered cola.
(   ) 5. They decided not to order the tofu dish because it has meat in it.
(   ) 6. They requested fast service because they were in a hurry.

B. Dialogue II
(   ) 1. The dining-room serves Chinese food only.
(   ) 2. The sweet-and-sour fish is sold out.
(   ) 3. The student ordered a cucumber salad dish in addition to the fish dish.
(   ) 4. The student spent more than fifteen dollars on the lunch.
(   ) 5. The dining-room staff member recommended cucumber salad because it tastes very good.
(   ) 6. The dining-room staff member discovered that the student paid him one dollar too much.

Section Two (Listen to the tape for the workbook)

A. Narrative (True/False)

(   ) 1. Wang Peng likes dumplings the best in the Chinese restaurant.
(   ) 2. Wang Peng arrived in the States two months ago.
(   ) 3. Wang Peng is not used to American food.
(   ) 4. Wang Peng is a good cook.
(   ) 5. Wang Peng likes the hot-and-sour soup in the restaurant very much.

B. Dialogue I (Multiple choice)

(   ) 1. Why did the man not drink any beer?
    a. He had to drive.
    b. He had to go to class.
    c. He had drunk too much beer already.

(   ) 2. What did he finally get from the woman?
    a. A bottle of coke.
    b. A glass of coke.
    c. A can of coke.

C. Dialogue II (Multiple choice)

(   ) 1. What is the relationship between the man and the woman?
        a. Husband/wife   b. Customer/waitress
        c. Father/daughter   d. Brother/sister

(   ) 2. Which of the following was NOT mentioned in the conversation?
        a. tofu   b. soup   c. beer   d. rice

(   ) 3. What did the man order for his meal?
        a. A tofu dish, a fish dish, and a soup
        b. A fish dish, a soup, and rice
        c. A fish dish, a beef dish, and a soup
        d. A tofu dish, a soup, and rice

II. Speaking Exercises

Section One (Answer the questions in Chinese based on the dialogues)

A. Dialogue I
1. How did the waiter greet the customers when they entered the restaurant?
2. Did the customers order any meat dishes? Why?
3. Please name all the food items they ordered in the restaurant?
4. Did they order any drinks? Why did the woman ask the waiter to rush?

B. Dialogue II
1. What did the dining-room staff member say about the fish dish?
2. What was the reason for the dining-room staff member to recommend the cucumber dish?
3. Please give the price for each of the food items that the student ordered.
4. What did the student say after receiving the changes?

Section two
A. You and your friends are in a Chinese restaurant. You like different kinds of food. So you discuss with the waiter about what to order. It turns out that everyone enjoys the food. Each student may play a role.

B. After the dinner, you and your friends discuss how to pay the bill. When the bill comes, you find that the waiter has over-charged you one dollar. You talk to the waiter about it.

III. Reading Comprehension

Section One

A. Answer the following questions about the dialogues.

Dialogue I

1. 谁吃素？

2. 他们点了些什么菜？

3. 王先生喝的东西跟李小姐喝的东西一样吗？他们喝什么？

4. 你觉得他们饿吗？为什么？

Dialogue II

1. 这个学生今天晚上想吃中餐还是西餐？

2. 他点了哪两个菜？

3. 一两米饭多少钱？

4. 学生给了师傅多少钱？

5. 师傅多给了学生多少钱？

B. Read the passage and answer the questions. (True/False)

　　今天中午老张请老王到餐馆吃饭。老张要老王点菜，老王不吃肉，所以点了一个家常豆腐，还点了一个凉拌黄瓜。这些菜很便宜。老张不知道老王不吃肉，所以点了一盘牛肉，还有一盘糖醋鱼。这些菜都很贵。菜上来了，老张想让老王吃贵的菜，所以他吃了很多豆腐和黄瓜。吃完饭以后，盘子里还有很多鱼和牛肉，可是老王还觉得很饿。

( ) 1. 今天的午饭是老王请客。
( ) 2. 老张和老王一共点了四个菜。
( ) 3. 老张点的菜很便宜。
( ) 4. 吃午饭的时候，老张才知道老王不吃肉。
( ) 5. 老张吃了很多豆腐和黄瓜，因为他也不喜欢吃肉。
( ) 6. 吃饭以后，盘子里还有很多豆腐和黄瓜。
( ) 7. 老王没有吃牛肉和鱼。

C. Read the following and answer the questions. (Multiple choice)

美味快餐店

菜		汤	
1. 宫保鸡丁	$5.95	1. 蛋花汤	$2.95
2. 红烧牛肉	$6.50	2. 酸辣汤	$2.95
3. 炒鱼片	$6.50	3. 鸡丝汤	$2.50
4. 京都排骨	$4.95	4. 豆腐湯	$1.50
5. 家常豆腐	$3.95		

( ) 1. This restaurant provides _____.
　　　a. buffet　　　b. banquet　　　c. fast food　　　d. free delivery

( ) 2. 要是你只有五块五毛钱，你想吃一菜一汤，你可以点_____。
　　　a. 炒鱼片、豆腐汤　　　　　　b. 家常豆腐、鸡丝汤
　　　c. 京都排骨、蛋花汤　　　　　d. 家常豆腐、豆腐汤

D. Read the note below and answer the questions. (True/False)

小王：

　　小张刚才给你打电话，想请你跟你太太这个星期六去他们家吃饺子。他现在在他的办公室。请你回来以后，给他打个电话。

　　　　　　　　　　　　　　　　　　小李

　　　　　　　　　　　　　　　　　　三点十分

（　　）1. 小张想请小王一个人吃饭。

（　　）2. 这个星期六小张要去饭馆吃饺子。

（　　）3. 小张要小王给他打电话。

（　　）4. 小张现在不在家。

（　　）5. 小王三点十分给小李打电话。

E. Translate the note above into English.

IV. Writing and Grammar Exercises

Section One

A. Following the model, rewrite the sentences below.

> Example: 我今年夏天没有看电影。
> ===>我今年夏天一个电影都(也)没有看。

1. 他今天早上没有吃东西。

2. 饭馆里人很多，没有位子了。

3. 我最近忙极了，没有时间。

4. 这篇课文的生词又多又难，我不懂。

5. 昨天晚上我忙极了，没睡觉。

B. Answer the following questions.

1. *A：* 你觉得是中餐好吃还是西餐好吃？

   B： _____ 。

2. *A：* 要是你不能吃味精，你可以跟服务员说什么？

   B： _____ 。

3. *A：* 今天我请客，你要点些什么菜？

   B： _____ 。

4. *A：* 要是你饿极了，你可以跟服务员说什么？

   B： _____ 。

5. *A：* 在美国是吃饭以前喝酒，还是吃饭以后喝酒？

   B： _____ 。

6. *A：* 天气热的时候，你喜欢吃什么？喝什么？

   B： _____ 。

C. Fill in the blanks, using the English in the parentheses as a clue:

A： 两杯啤酒三块八，一瓶可乐一块钱，_____ (total) 四块八。

B： 这是十块钱。

A： _____ (give you change) 六块二。

*B：*谢谢。哦，_____ (you gave the wrong change)。应该找我五块二，

可是你_____ (you gave me one dollar too much)。

D. Fill in the blanks with proper resultative complements:

1. 爸爸：小明，功课做得怎么样了？

   小明：功课还没做_____。

2. *A:* 老师说的话你听_____了吗？

   B: 老师说话说得太快，我没_____。

3. *A:* 师傅，还有酸辣汤吗？

   B: 对不起，已经卖_____了。

4. 这个字不对，你写_____了。

E. Complete and expand the dialogue:

男客人：_____？

服务生：对不起，糖醋鱼没有了，红烧牛肉可以吗？

男客人：也可以。

服务生：除了红烧牛肉以外，_____？

女客人：老王，_____？

男客人：好，_____。

服务生：一盘红烧牛肉，两碗酸辣汤，_____？

男客人：_____。

女客人：我不要米饭。

F. Translate the following sentences into Chinese.

1. Bring us two glasses of beer. (来)

2. Do you want to have dinner at home or go to a restaurant? (想; 还是)

3. *A:* How many classes do you have today?

   B: I don't have a single class today. (一...都/也...)

4. *A:* Do you have any Japanese books?

   B: No, I don't have any single Japanese book. (一...都/也...)

5. Waiter: Do you want anything else?

   Customer: Yes, give me a bottle of cola, please. (来)

6. *A:* How do you like the hot-and-sour soup? (觉得)

B: It's a bit sour and a bit hot. Very tasty. (reduplication of adj.)

7. The beef braised in soy sauce is extremely good. Why don't you buy one? (. . . 极了)

8. This book is extremely interesting.

9. *A:* Did I write this character right? (resultative complement)

   B: No, you wrote it wrong. (resultative complement)

10. Sorry! Sweet-and-sour fish is sold out!

11. The home-style tofu is extremely tasty! (. . . 极了)

12. You gave me fifty cents too much for the change.

Lesson Thirteen   At the Library

I. Listening Comprehension

Section One (Listen to the tape for the textbook)

A. Dialogue I (Multiple choice)

(   ) 1. What does the student wish to borrow?
      a. books   b. tapes   c. records   d. dictionaries

(   ) 2. What did the student bring to the library?
      a. a student ID   b. a library card
      c. a credit card   d. a book

(   ) 3. When did the student talk to the library staff?
      a. 4:30   b. 5:00   c. 5:30   d. 8:00

(   ) 4. What is downstairs in the library?
      a. a reading room   b. a reference room
      c. a language lab   d. a computer room

B. Dialogue II (True/False)

(   ) 1. This library is an open-shelf library.
(   ) 2. When checking out books, you need to present your library card as well as your student ID.
(   ) 3. You can check out a book for eight months at a time at this library.
(   ) 4. The overdue penalty is fifty cents per day.
(   ) 5. You can only check out dictionaries on weekends.

Section Two (Listen to the tape for the workbook)

A. Narrative (True/False)

(   ) 1. In a Chinese college library, the students have to ask the librarian to look for the books they want to borrow.
(   ) 2. In a Chinese college library, a student does not need any ID to check out books.
(   ) 3. In a Chinese college library, a student cannot renew the books he/she checked out.

B. Dialogue (True/False)

(   ) 1. The conversation took place inside the library.
(   ) 2. No audiotapes are allowed to leave the library.
(   ) 3. The man is a teacher.
(   ) 4. The man wishes to check out some audiotapes.
(   ) 5. The language lab is right next door to the library.

II. Speaking Exercises

Section One (Answer the questions in Chinese based on the texts)

A. Dialogue I
1. What does the man wish to borrow?
2. Where is the language lab?
3. What did the man forget to bring?
4. Did the man bring any ID with him?
5. How late does the language lab stay open?
6. When did the conversation take place?

B. Dialogue II
1. What does the man wish to borrow?
2. Is the man allowed to go in the stacks to look for books? How do you know?
3. What does the man need to have to borrow books?
4. What will happen to the man if he fails to return books on time?
5. Can he borrow dictionaries?

Section Two

A. You are studying Chinese in China. You go to the library to borrow books, but you don't know how to check out a book. You ask the librarian for help. You would like to know how many books you can check out each time, how long you can keep the books, and what identification you need for checking out books.

B. Ask your friend if you can check out videotapes from the language lab, how long you can keep the tapes each time, what ID you need to check out tapes and if you can renew them.

C. Tell a story based on the picture below.

III. Reading Comprehension

Section One (Answer the questions about the dialogues)

A. Dialogue I

1. 这个学生要借什么？

2. 学生可以把录音带借回家吗？你怎么知道？

3. 学生和职员在哪儿说话？

4. 学生忘了什么？

5. 学生带了什么证件？

6. 图书馆开到几点？

7. 他们说话的时候是几点钟？

8. 学生今天借到了他要的东西吗？你怎么知道？

B. Dialogue II

1. 这个学生要借什么？

2. 学生可以自己进去找他要的东西吗？

3. 学生借书的时候得用什么证件？

4. 书可以借多久？

5. 要是过期两天得罚多少钱？

6. 书可以续借吗？

7. 学生可以把字典借回家吗？

Section Two

A. Read the following passage and answer the questions. (True/False)

在美国的大学图书馆借书，老师，研究生和大学生一次可以借的时间不一样。老师可以借一年，研究生可以借半年，大学生只能借一个月。借的书，要是没有人借，可以续借，很方便。

( ) 1. 老师一次借书可以借十二个月。
( ) 2. 老师，研究生和大学生借了书都可以续借。
( ) 3. 大学生一次只可以借一本书。
( ) 4. 如果一位大学生借一本书要借十个星期他得续借两次。
( ) 5. 研究生借书可以比大学生多借四个月。

B. Read the following passage and answer the questions. (True/False)

老师说要想中文进步得快，最好的办法就是每天都听录音。他告诉我们中文录音带都在语言实验室，但是不能借回家去，只能在那儿听。语言实验室除了星期六以外每天都开。而且早上七点半就开门，晚上九点半才关门。老师还告诉我们去借录音带的时候不要忘了带借书证。

( ) 1. 老师觉得听录音带是学中文的好办法。
( ) 2. 学生可以把录音带借回家听。
( ) 3. 语言实验室一星期开五天。
( ) 4. 早上八点一刻，语言实验室已经开了。
( ) 5. 借录音带的时候要看学生证。

IV. Writing and Grammar Exercises

Section One

A. Following the model, rewrite each of the sentences below into one that contains the 把 structure.

>   Example: 我带来了你的一本书。

>   ===>我把你的那本书带来了。

1. 我还给了图书馆一本书。

2. 他开走了王朋的汽车。

3. 他借回来了录音带。

4. 他写错了字。

5. 我看完了这本书。

6. 你没有给我你的借书证。

7. 他给了女朋友一张电影票。

8. 我买回来了一个电脑。

B. Complete the following sentences with 如果/要是.

1. 如果你没有字典，_____。

2. 如果你借的书过期了，_____。

3. 如果你想学好中文，_____。

4. 要是你找不到你要的书，_____。

5. 要是你忘了带证件，_____。

C. Fill in the blanks using the clue in the parentheses.

1. 请你在餐厅 _____ (wait for a while).

2. 请问，这本书可以 _____ (how long can I borrow)?

3. 请你把录音带_____ (return to the library).

4. 你把学生证 _____
   (Where did you put your student ID) ?

D. Answer the following questions using 把.
1. *A:* 我的中文书在哪儿？

   B: _____。（放在）

2. (正在吃饭)

A: 妈妈，我可以出去玩吗？

B: _____。(吃完)

3. A: 已经十二点了，快睡觉吧！

B: _____。(预习好)

4. A: 你借的录音带在哪儿？我想听一下。

B: 那盘录音带明天就过期了，_____。(还给)

E. Put the following sentences into the correct order.

1. 在学生餐厅   今天早上   我   一杯   喝了   咖啡。

2. 跟小李   他   打球   昨天下午   一个钟头   打了。

3. 我弟弟   写了   用中文   昨天晚上   写信   三十分钟。

4. 王老师   二十分钟   第一节课   教了   教发音。

F. Translate the following sentences into Chinese.

1. He ate his breakfast for two hours, and did not finish it until 10 o'clock. (duration; V + 到)

2. They danced for five hours last night. (duration)

3. *A:* You wrote this character wrong. How long have you studied Chinese?

   B: Twenty years. But only for one week each year. (duration)

4. Would you wait here for a little while? (能不能 ，V+一下)

5. Please put your library card on the table.

6. I waited for my girlfriend's phone call until eleven o'clock last night.

7. I returned the dictionary to her this morning. (把)

8. The language laboratory is upstairs.

9. Do you have any other ID in addition to a student ID? (除了... 以外)

10. How late does the library stay open? (V + 到)

Section Two

A. Write a letter to a library in Chinese to find out how to borrow books, how many books you can check out at a time and for how long, and what the fine is if the books are overdue.

B. Write a note to your Chinese friend, explaining to him/her how to borrow tapes at your language lab.

Lesson Fourteen   Asking Directions

I. Listening Comprehension

Section One (Listen to the tape for the textbook)

A. Dialogue I (Multiple choice)

(   ) 1. Where is the man going?
      a. library   b. student activities center   c. computer center   d. bookstore

(   ) 2. Where is the woman going?
      a. library   b. student activities center   c. computer center   d. bookstore

(   ) 3. Which of the following places is the closest to the bookstore?
      a. athletic field b. computer center c. student activities center   d. library

(   ) 4. Which of the following places is the farthest away from the two speakers?
      a. athletic field b. computer center c. student activities center   d. library

B. Dialogue II (True/False)
(   ) 1. The man has never been to Chinatown.
(   ) 2. The woman is asking the man to give her a ride.
(   ) 3. The woman has a map.
(   ) 4. According to the dialogue, they finally get to Chinatown.

Section Two (Listen to the tape for the workbook)

A. Dialogue I   (True/False)
(   ) 1. The library is to the north of the dormitory.
(   ) 2. The woman now knows where she took a wrong turn a moment ago.
(   ) 3. To get to the library, the woman needs to make a right turn first, then a left turn.
(   ) 4. There is no traffic light between the dormitory and the library.

B. Narrative (Listen to the narrative and identify the buildings in the picture on p.24.)

(   ) 1. Dormitory
(   ) 2. Library
(   ) 3. Student activities center
(   ) 4. Computer center
(   ) 5. Classroom

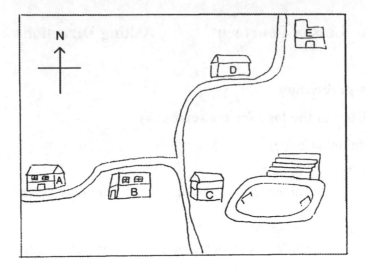

II. Speaking Exercises

Section One (Answer the questions in Chinese based on the texts.)

A. Dialogue I
1. Where is Mr. Jin going?
2. Has Mr. Jin been to the computer center before? Please explain.
3. Which one is farther, the computer center or the sports field?
4. Where is the computer center?
5. Where is Miss Tian going?
6. Why did Mr. Jin say that had he known it earlier, he would not have asked for the directions?

B. Dialogue II
1. Does Old Wang know how to get to Chinatown? Please explain.
2. Who has a map, Old Wang or Old Li?
3. Where were the speakers at the beginning of the conversation, north of Chinatown or south of Chinatown?
4. How many intersections do they need to pass before they reach Chinatown?
5. What did they do when they found out that the street which they were supposed to turn onto was a one-way street?
6. Did they eventually reach Chinatown? Please explain.

Section Two

A. You are a new student at a Chinese school. Ask your fellow student how to get to the classroom from the dormitory. And find out the locations of the library and the student union in relation to the classroom.

B. Your Chinese roommate has just arrived on campus. Please explain to her/him how to get to the library, the student activities center, and the athletic field from the dormitory.

III. Reading Comprehension

Section One (Answer the questions about the dialogues)

A. Dialogue I

1. 老金想去哪里？

2. 他知道怎么走吗？

3. 电脑中心旁边有什么？

4. 书店在哪儿？

5. 为什么金先生，田小姐要一起走？

B. Dialogue II

1. 老王要去哪里？

2. 为什么他要老李告诉他怎么走？

3. 为什么第四个路口只能往左拐？

4. 最后老王和老李到了什么地方？

Section Two

A. Read the following passage and answer the questions.

> 小田家离学校很远。每天早上，他得走十五分钟到火车站，再坐一小时火车到台南。学校就在火车站旁边，下火车后，不用走太久。因为走路和坐火车上学得花很多时间，所以他想下学期在学校住。

1. 小田住在台南吗？你怎么知道？

2. 小田每天上学要花多少时间？

3. 小田下火车后要走很久吗？为什么？

4. 为什么小田想在学校住？

B. Read the following passage and answer the questions.

> 老李在纽约住了八年了，周末常常到中国城去买东西、吃中国饭。因为每次去中国城都是坐朋友的车，所以有一次他自己开车到中国城去就迷路了。最后只好去问人，别人告诉他怎么走以后，他就找到了。

1. 老李知道怎么去中国城吗？你怎么知道？

2. 老李常去中国城做什么？

3. 最后老李怎么找到了中国城？

C. Answer the following true-or-false questions according to the map.

( ) 1. 公园在老金家的东边。

( ) 2. 医院在电影院的南边。

( ) 3. 图书馆在医院的西边。

( ) 4. 公园的北边有车站。

( ) 5. 饭店离老金家很近。

( ) 6. 学校和电影院的中间是书店。

D. Fill in the letters according to the given information.

宿舍在车站的南边。宿舍的西边是图书馆。电影院在图书馆的西北边。学生活动中心在电影院和公园的中间。医院在宿舍的南边。

a: 图书馆   b: 宿舍   c: 电影院   d: 学生活动中心   e: 医院

IV. Writing and Grammar Exercises

Section One

A. Make questions using the given words, and also answer the questions.

Example: 学校/ 中国城

===>学校离中国城远不远？

===> 学校离中国城不远。

1. 宿舍/ 学生活动中心。

===>

===>

2. 图书馆/ 运动场。

===>

===>

3. 书店 / 电脑中心。

===>

===>

4. 你的家 / 电影院。

==>

==>

5. 美国 / 中国。

==>

==>

6. 上海 / 台北。

==>

==>

B. Follow the model and make comparative sentences using the given words.

Example: 英文 / 日文 = = = > 英文没有日文那么难。/ 英文比日文容易。

1. 说中文 / 写汉字

2. 住在宿舍 / 住在家里

3. 学校的饭 / 饭馆的饭

4. 东京 / 台北

5. 走路 / 开车

6. 男孩子 / 女孩子

C. Answer the following questions using the English phrase in the parentheses as a clue.

1. *A:* 学校的书店在哪里？

   B: _____ (inside the student union)。

2. *A:* 我的书哪儿去了？

   B: _____ (under the table)。

3. *A:* 请问运动场离这儿远不远？

   B: 不远，_____

      (just between the computer center and the library) 。

4. *A:* 你的宿舍在哪儿？

   B: _____ (beside the school's bookstore) 。

5. *A:* 我们到哪儿去打球？

   B: _____

      (the sports field outside the classroom) 。

D. Answer the following questions using the given words and sentence pattern.

      Sentence pattern: 一直往_____，到_____，往_____就到了。

1. 请问到学校的书店怎么走？(南，第二个路口，西)

2. 到电影院怎么走？(前，第三个红绿灯，右)

3. 请问到运动场怎么走？(东，图书馆，北)

4. 到中国城怎么走？(前，有中国字的地方，左。)

E. Answer the following questions using 过.

        Example: 台北夏天热不热？

            ===> 我不知道，因为我没去过台北。

1. 日文语法难不难？

2. 上海人多不多？

3. 那个中国电影好看吗？

4. 跳舞有意思吗？

5. 红叶好看吗？

F. Fill in the blanks with resultative complements.

1. 老师说的语法你听＿＿＿＿＿＿＿＿了吗？

2. 老师，这个汉字我没写＿＿＿＿＿＿＿，您再看看。

3. 今天看电影的人很多，我没买＿＿＿＿＿＿＿＿电影票。

4. 妹妹说她写＿＿＿＿＿＿＿＿信就跟我去打球。

5. 你去中国的机票买＿＿＿＿＿＿＿＿了吗？

G. Use the given words to make sentences with the expression "一 . . . 就 . . ."

   Example: 我回家以后就开始预习功课。

   ===> 我一回家就预习功课。

1. 今天我起床以后就听录音。

2. 这一课很容易，我看了一下就懂了。

3. 活动中心不远，往前走到路口，再往左拐就到了。

4. 这本书很多人想借，请你看完就还给我。

5. 我给妈妈买了一件衣服，买好了就给她了。

H. Translate the following into Chinese.

1. The language laboratory is very far from here.（离）

2. Have you ever seen that videotape?（过）

3. Walk straight north and you will get to the computer center.（一直，就）

4. *A:* Is the library far away from the athletic field?（离）

   B: The library is not that far.（那么）

5. Go straight north from your dorm, make a left turn at the first intersection, and you will be there.（一直，往...拐，就）

6. Her Japanese is very good. She has read many Japanese books.（过）

7. I'll go shopping if it's a nice day tomorrow. (就)

8. If next week is colder than this week, I'll study in the library. (比，就)

9. As soon as I find the dictionary, I'll give you a call. (一...就)

10. I understood him the moment he said it. (一...就)

11. He went to the sports field to play ball.

12. Were you able to buy that book successfully?

Section Two

A. Draw a map of your school campus labeling it in Chinese, and describe the best way to get to the library, the student activities center, and the computer center from your dormitory.

B. Write a paragraph telling your Chinese friend how to get to your home / dormitory from the airport / bus stop / train station.

Lesson Fifteen   Birthday Party

I. Listening Comprehension

Section One (Listen to the tape for the textbook)

A. Dialogue I (Multiple choice)

(   ) 1. What was Wang Peng doing when Li You called him?
    a. dancing   b. singing   c. eating   d. reading

(   ) 2. When is Little Lin's birthday?
    a. yesterday b. today   c. tomorrow d. day after tomorrow

(   ) 3. What time will the party start?
    a. 7:00   b. 8:00   c. 9:00   d. 10:00

(   ) 4. What will Wang Peng bring to the party?
    a. snacks   b. soda   c. fruit   d. juice

(   ) 5. How will Wang Peng get to the party?
    a. by driving his own car   b. by bus
    c. by riding in Li You's car   d. by walking

B. Dialogue II (Multiple choice)

(   ) 1. Whose birthday was it?
    a. Wang Peng's   b. Li You's
    c. Little Lin's   d. Helen's

(   ) 2. Whom did Wang Peng meet at the party?
    a. Little Lin's cousin   b. Li You's cousin
    c. Little Lin's sister   d. Li You's sister

(   ) 3. What is Tom's sign in the Chinese Zodiac?
    a. dog   b. ox   c. horse   d. tiger

(   ) 4. Why will Tom be handsome in the future?
    a. His father is handsome   b. His mother is pretty
    c. Tom has a beautiful nose d. Tom has beautiful eyes

(   ) 5. What shall Tom study in the future?
    a. Chinese b. English   c. piano   d. violin

Section Two (Listen to the tape for the workbook) (Multiple choice)

A. Dialogue I (Multiple choice)
(   ) 1. This dialogue is most likely to have occurred_____.
    a. at a birthday party
    b. on the phone
    c. in a classroom

39

(   ) 2. Which of the following statements is true?
   a. Li You does not know what day tomorrow is.
   b. Li You does not know what date tomorrow is.
   c. Li You is not asking what day or what date tomorrow is.

(   ) 3. How did Li You discover that it is Wang Peng's birthday?
   a. He told her earlier in her car.
   b. She learned that from his student ID.
   c. She learned that from some of his friends.

(   ) 4. Wang Peng says that he did not know that the next day was his birthday because he _____.
   a. had been too busy and forgot about it.
   b. did not want to celebrate his birthday.
   c. was confused about the day's date.

(   ) 5. What are they going to do at tomorrow's party?
   a. have dinner and then dance.
   b. have a reception followed by a dinner.
   c. have dinner and then watch a movie.

B. Dialogue (Multiple choice)

(   ) 1. Why were they talking about Wang Peng's parents?
   Because _____ .
   a. they showed up at the party.
   b. they sent their recent photo to Wang Peng.
   c. they appear in a photo that was taken many years ago.

(   ) 2. According to the dialogue, who does Wang Peng take after?
   a. His mother.
   b. His father.
   c. Both his parents.

II. Speaking Exercises

Section One (Answer the questions in Chinese based on the texts)

A. Dialogue I

1. Why did Li You talk to Wang Peng?
2. What will happen at Little Lin's home tonight? Please provide as many details as possible.
3. Who will go to Little Lin's home tonight?
4. What will Wang Peng bring to Little Lin's house?
5. Why didn't Wang Peng want Li You to give him a ride?

5. Why didn't Wang Peng want Li You to give him a ride?

B. Dialogue II

1. Who asked about Wang Peng before he arrived? Why?
2. What did Wang Peng say to Little Lin when he entered Little Lin's house? How did Little Lin reply?
3. Did Wang Peng arrive early or late? How do you know?
4. Did Wang Peng meet anyone at Little Lin's house?
5. What did Li You tell Helen about Wang Peng?
6. Does Helen speak Chinese? Please explain.
7. Who is Tom? What can you tell us about him? Can you describe Tom's appearance?
8. Why did Li You say that Tom should study piano? Please explain.

Section Two

A. Describe one of your friends or relatives, including his or her age, personality, appearance, family background, hobbies, etc.

B. Call your friend or relative, invite him/her to a party, and tell him/her what the arrangements are. Tell him/her how to get to your house. Each of your classmates may play a role.

C. Tell a story based on the picture below.

III. Reading Comprehension

Section One (Answer the questions about the dialogues)

A. Dialogue I

1. 李友打电话给王朋的时候，他正在做什么？

2. 李友今天晚上七点钟有什么事？

3. 小林是男的还是女的？

4. 开舞会以前他们先做什么？

5. 为什么王朋要带果汁？

6. 谁要走路去小林家？为什么？

B. Dialogue II

1. 王朋为什么去小林家？

2. 王朋送给小林什么？

3. 海伦是谁？汤姆是谁？汤姆多大？

4. 海伦是王朋的同学，对不对？你怎么知道？

5. 海伦是在哪儿学的中文？

6. 为什么小林说汤姆将来一定很帅？

7. 汤姆长得像谁？

8. 汤姆将来会很高吗？

9. 汤姆将来应该学什么？为什么？

10. 汤姆是属什么的？

Section Two

A. Read the following passage and answer the questions. (True/False)

昨天是小金二十岁生日，晚上我们在他的宿舍给他过生日。大家给他买了一张卡片。小金的女朋友买了果汁，汽水（儿），还有很多好吃的东西。大家一边吃东西一边玩，一直玩到十二点多才回家，所以我的功课没做完，今天的考试也考得糟糕极了。

( ) 1. 小金今年二十岁。

( ) 2. 小金跟他的爸爸妈妈一起住在家里。

( ) 3. 生日卡，果汁和汽水（儿）都是大家一起买的。

( ) 4. 昨天大家很晚才回家。

( ) 5. 今天的考试小金考得很不好。

B. Read the following passage and answer the questions. (True/False)

小高很喜欢她日文班的一个很帅的男同学。那个男同学跟小高一样，是美国人。他的眼睛是蓝色的，鼻子高高的，笑的时候很好看。他又会唱歌又会弹钢琴。下个星期六学校有个舞会，小高很想请他一起去跳舞，可是不好意思问他。

( ) 1. 小高喜欢的男学生也学日文。

( ) 2. 小高是美国人。

( ) 3. 那个男同学的眼睛是黑色的。

( ) 4. 下个星期六小高家裏有个舞会。

( ) 5. 那个男同学请小高跟他去跳舞。

IV. Writing and Grammar Exercises

Section One

A. Following the English directions, use the structures "是 . . . 的" or "了" to ask and answer questions based on the passage below.

王朋和李友昨天晚上从学校开车到电影院去看电影。看完电影以后，他们走路到电影院附近的一个中国饭馆去吃晚饭。吃饭的时候他们喝了一点儿酒。

1. Find out if Wang Peng went to the movies last night.

    Q: _____ 。

    A: _____ 。

2. Find out who went together with Wang Peng.

    Q: _____ 。

    A: _____ 。

3. Find out how they went to the movie theater.

    Q: _____ 。

    A: _____ 。

4. Find out from where they went to the movie theater.

    Q: _____ 。

A: _____ 。

5. Find out if Wang Peng and Li You ate dinner last night.

   Q: _____ 。

   A: _____ 。

6. Find out where Wang Peng and Li You ate dinner last night.

   Q: _____ 。

   A: _____ 。

7. Find out how Wang Peng and Li You went to the restaurant.

   Q: _____ 。

   A: _____ 。

8. Find out if Wang Peng and Li You drank last night.

   Q: _____ 。

   A: _____ 。

9. Find out where Wang Peng and Li You drank wine last night.

   Q: _____ 。

   A: _____ 。

B. Fill in the appropriate blanks with 了、过 or 是...的. Put X in the blanks which do not need to be filled.

1. *A:* 小张_____来_____吗？

   B: 来了。

   A: 小张_____什麼时候来_____？

   B: 昨天晚上来_____。

   A: 小张_____以前来_____吗？

   B: 没有。

2. *A:* 这是你的书吧？

   B: 对，是我的。

   A: 你_____什麼时候买_____？

   B: 去年买_____。

   A: 在哪儿买_____？

   B: 在中国买_____，你看_____这本书吗？

   A: 没看_____，我以前不知道有这本书。

C. Complete the following sentences using 一定.

1. 你的弟弟从小喜欢运动，_____。(athlete)

2. 这个学生又会中文，又会英文，又会法文，_____。(smart)

3. 他平常不喜欢练习说中文，也不喜欢练习写汉字，_____。
   (in a terrible mess)

4. 他父亲天天去中国饭馆吃饭，_____。(like)

D. Use the pivotal construction "Noun + Verb + Noun + Verb" to ask and answer
   questions about the underlined part in each of the following sentences. You can use
   the following verbs: 让，请，叫，要

        Example: 妈妈   妹妹   <u>学钢琴</u>/ <u>看电视</u>

             ===> *A:* 妈妈让妹妹做什么？

                  B: 妈妈让妹妹学钢琴。

             ===> *C:* 妈妈不让妹妹做什么？

                  D: 妈妈不让妹妹看电视。

1. 老师   学生   在语言实验室<u>看录像</u>/ <u>聊天儿</u>

   A:

   B:

   C:

   D:

2. 图书管理员   我   把<u>证件</u>给他/ 把<u>字典</u>带回家。

   A:

   B:

   C:

   D:

3. 父母   我   用<u>中文</u>给他们写信/ 用<u>英文</u>给他们写信

   A:

   B:

C:

D:

4. 医生   我哥哥   多吃水果/ 喝酒

    A:

    B:

    C:

    D:

E. Answer the following questions, using the "正在 . . . 呢" structure.

1. *A:* 今天早上六点，你在做什么？我给你打电话，可是没人接。(take a bath)

    B:

2. *A:* 我昨天下午三点来你家，你不在。你上哪儿去了？(take an exam)

    B:

3. *A:* 明天早上九点钟你有事吗？你开车带我去买东西可以吗？(attend a class)

    B:

4. (打电话)
    A: 你正在做什么呢？(watch T.V.)

    B:

F. Following the model, combine each pair of sentences into one.

     Example: 我妈妈作了一个菜。 那个菜很好吃。

              ===> 我妈妈作了一个很好吃的菜。

1. 王朋给李友写了一封信。 那封信很客气。

2. 我姐姐昨天买了一件新衣服。 那件衣服很好看。

3. 黄先生上个星期认识了一个朋友。 那个朋友在日本工作。

4. 小张借了一本书。 那本书又难懂又没有意思。

5. 我有一个表姐。 她会弹钢琴。

G. Complete the following sentences using 还.

1. A: 我们出去打球好吗？

   B: 等一下，_____。（吃饭）

2. （打电话）

   A: 喂，王朋在家吗？

   B: 他在家，可是_____。（起床）

3. A: 你怎麽不睡觉？

   B: 我不能睡，_____。（功课）

4. A: 李友回来了吗？

   B: 没有，_____。（在小林家跳舞）

H. Translate the following into Chinese.

1. I will eat first and then go to play ball. (先 . . . 再. . .)

2. The girl who danced with you last night was my cousin.

3. I will go to China for sure in the future. (将来，一定)

4. It's already 10:30.   How come Little Lin still hasn't come.

5. We had our dancing party at my boyfriend's home. (是. . . 的)

6. Who gave you this birthday present? (是. . . 的)

7. She either plays the piano or goes to dance on weekends; she doesn't like to watch TV. (或者)

8. What is the salesperson saying? (在. . . 呢)

9. My younger brother asked me to call him tomorrow. (pivotal sentence)

10. Her eyes are big and her nose is high, and she looks very much like her mother. (reduplication of adj: 像)

11. Where did you meet him? (认识，是...的)

12. How old is your younger sister? What is her sign in the Chinese zodiac? (属)

Section Two

A. Write a letter inviting your friend to attend your birthday party. Tell him/her what activities you will have at the party. Don't forget to tell him/her the date, time and place.

B. Write a paragraph describing the appearance of a family member. Make sure that you describe his/her eyes, nose, height, legs, fingers, etc.

Lesson Sixteen   Seeing a Doctor

I. Listening Comprehension

Section One (Listen to the tape for the textbook) (Multiple choice)

A. Dialogue I (Multiple choice)
(   ) 1. Why did the man go to see the doctor?
        a. He had a cold.
        b. He had a stomachache.
        c. He injured his hand.
        e. He injured his leg.

(   ) 2. What caused the man's problem?
        a. Insufficient sleep.
        b. A basketball game.
        c. A soccer match.
        d. Leftover food.

(   ) 3. What is the treatment for the man's problem?
        a. To take a shot and some medicine.
        b. To stay home and rest.
        c. To have physical therapy and take medicine.
        d. To take medicine only.

(   ) 4. How many pills does the man need to take daily?
        a. 2
        b. 3
        c. 5
        d. 6

(   ) 5. What is the doctor's suggestion to the man?
        a. stop playing basketball for three months.
        b. no more soccer games.
        c. fast for one day.
        d. drink plenty of liquids.

B. Dialogue II
(   ) 1. The woman cried because she was homesick.
(   ) 2. The man is allergic to flowers.
(   ) 3. The woman will go to the pharmacy tomorrow to buy four kinds of medicine.
(   ) 4. The man advised the woman to go to see a doctor right away.
(   ) 5. The woman has no health insurance.
(   ) 6. The woman is a doctor.

Section Two (Listen to the tape for the workbook)

A. Dialogue I (True/False)

(   ) 1. Li You has not seen Wang Peng for a few days.

(   ) 2. Wang Peng has been suffering from a cold these days.

(   ) 3. Wang Peng does not need to see the doctor because he has some Chinese
           medicine that he has brought from China.

(   ) 4. Wang Peng is feeling much better today.

B. Dialogue II (Multiple choice)

(   ) 1. According to the doctor, which of the following statements is true?
       a. The patient is seriously ill.
       b. The patient is not ill at all.
       c. The patient is ill, but the problem is not serious.

(   ) 2. What does the doctor think of the patient's dinner yesterday?
       a. He thinks the patient should have eaten three bowls of dumplings.
       b. He thinks the patient should have eaten less rice but more beef.
       c. He thinks the patient should not have eaten so much.

(   ) 3. How many tablets is the patient supposed to take daily?
       a. 3   b. 6   c. 9

C. Narrative (True/False)

(   ) 1. In China, people go to see a doctor only when they are seriously ill.

(   ) 2. In China, a doctor's consultation is inexpensive, but the prices for medicine are
           extremely high.

(   ) 3. Medical insurance in the U.S. is very expensive because people go to see a doctor
           even for small ailments.

II. Speaking Exercises

Section One (Answer the questions in Chinese based on the texts)

A. Dialogue I

1. Why did the patient go to see the doctor?
2. What happened to the patient yesterday?
3. What did the doctor do after listening to the patient?
4. How is the doctor going to treat the patient?
5. How should the patient take the medicine?
6. What is the doctor's suggestion to the patient at the end of the consultation? Is the
    patient willing to do what the doctor recommended? Please explain.

B. Dialogue II

1. Why does Little Xie have red eyes?

2. How did Little Xie try to treat her allergy?
3. Why did the man ask Little Xie to see a doctor right away?
4. Is Little Xie willing to see a doctor? Please explain.

Section Two

A. You came home last night around nine o'clock, and were very hungry. You saw some leftover food on the table and you ate it. Around midnight you started to have a stomachache and you had to go to the bathroom many times throughout the night. Explain to your doctor what happened, and ask him/her if there is any medicine that you can take to treat your problem. Don't forget to ask the doctor how to take the medicine.

B. Call your teacher to tell him/her that you are not able to go to school because you caught a cold and are running a fever and have a bad cough.

C. Tell a story based on the picture below.

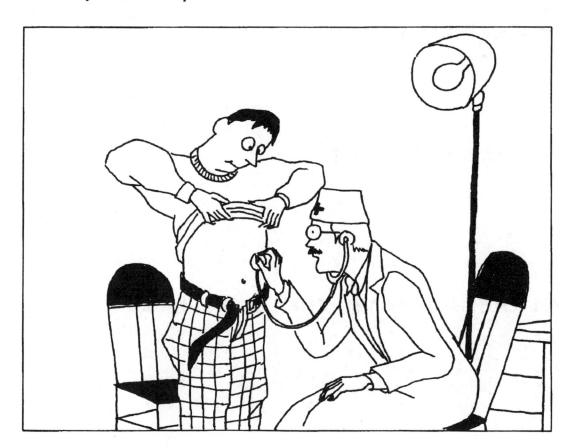

III. Reading Comprehension

Section One (Answer the questions about the dialogues)

A. Dialogue I

1. 病人什么地方不舒服？

2. 病人昨天吃什么东西了？

3. 医生说病人是什么病？

4. 病人得打针和吃药吗？药怎么吃？

5. 医生说最好的办法是什么？病人觉得那个办法好吗？为什么？

B. Dialogue II

1. 小谢为什么眼睛红红的？

2. 小谢的身体哪儿不舒服？怎么不舒服？

3. 小谢是在哪里买的药？

4. 小谢为什么买了四、五种药？

5. 小谢上次生病去看医生了没有？

6. 小谢为什么不去看医生？

Section Two

A. Read the following passage and answer the questions.(True/False)

因为今天要考试，小马昨天晚上看书看到今天早上四点才睡觉，六点就起床了。一起床他就觉得头有一点儿疼。吃早饭以后，小马头越来越疼，不能去上课。小马的妈妈带他去看医生。医生说小马没什么问题，只是睡觉不够，好好睡两天就会好了。医生没有给他打针，也没给他药吃。

( ) 1. 因为昨天小马考试考得不好，所以今天他头疼。
( ) 2. 妈妈带小马去看医生。
( ) 3. 小马没有病，只是睡觉不够。
( ) 4. 医生给了小马一些药，但是没给他打针。

B. Read the following passage and answer the questions. (True/False)

小钱住在学校外边，她喜欢自己做饭。但是这个星期她的功课很多，没有时间做饭，就每天到学校的餐厅吃饭。今天中午她吃了一盘红烧牛肉，还喝了一碗酸辣汤。虽然很便宜，可是不太好吃。回家以后她的肚子很不舒服，上了好几次厕所。下午她的肚子疼极了，就去看医生。医生说她吃坏肚子了。小钱说她以后不去餐厅吃饭了，还是自己做饭好。

( ) 1. 小钱住在学校的宿舍里。
( ) 2. 小钱去餐厅吃饭是因为她很不喜欢自己做饭。
( ) 3. 餐厅的饭又贵又不好吃。
( ) 4. 小钱肚子不舒服因为中午吃的饭有问题。
( ) 5. 医生叫小钱以后不要到餐厅去吃饭。

IV. Writing and Grammar Exercises

Section One

A. Fill in the blanks, using the English phrase in the parentheses as a clue.

1. 他上个星期 _____ 。(went to Chinatown twice)

2. 这种药 _____ ? (to take how many times per day)

3. 我弟弟肚子不舒服, 一个钟头就 _____ 。
   (went to the rest room several times)

4. 我和我的朋友想明年 _____ 。(go to Japan once)

5. 姐姐生病了, 我想 _____ 。 (go to see her once every day)

6. 老李 _____ 。(call his girl friend three times a day)

B. Translate the following expressions into Chinese.

1. please sit down:

2. please buy some fruit and bring it back:

3. please come in:

4. go upstairs:

5. take out a book:

6. run out of the dorm:

7. walk into the classroom:

8. go into the rest room:

9. come in the computer room:

10. walk downstairs:

C. Answer the following questions.

1. *A:* 你对什么药过敏？

   B: _____ 。

2. *A:* 谁对你最好？为什么？

   B: _____ 。

3. *A:* 哪些练习对你学中文有用？

   B: _____ 。

4. *A:* 喝酒对你身体好吗？为什么？

   B: _____ 。

5. *A:* 穿什么颜色的衣服对你最合适？

   B: _____ 。

D. Complete the following sentences using "要不然"

1. 你应该每天都听录音，_____ 。

2. 生了病应该赶快去看医生，_____ 。

3. 我明天有一个考试，我要复习一下，_____ 。

4. 你借的书要是到期了，就应该续借，_____ 。

5. 你要天天运动，_____ 。

E. Complete the following sentences with the expression "越来越".

      Example: 现在是十一月了，<u>天气越来越冷了</u>。（天气）

1. 第十课以後课文很难，因为 _____。
   (too many new words)

2. 我不想吃餐厅的饭了，因为 _____。
   (the food is getting worse)

3. 我每天都打球，所以 _____。
   (become healthier)

4. 我最近不太忙，因为 _____。
   (less homework)

5. 他比以前用功，所以 _____。
   (do better on tests)

F. Complete the following sentences using the expression 再说.

1. 我不喜欢吃剩菜，因为容易吃坏肚子，_____。
   (does not taste good)

2. 我想明年到中国去，因为老师说中国有很多好玩的地方，_____

   _____。 （can practice Chinese)

3. 我的哥哥喜欢吃中国饭，因为中国不太贵，_____。
   (delicious)

4. *A:* 这双鞋你喜欢不喜欢？

   B: 不喜欢，太贵，_____。(color)

5. *A:* 吃完晚饭以后，你要做什么？

   B: 我们打球去吧，几天没运动了，_____。
   (weather, comfortable)

G. Complete the following short dialogues.

1. *A:* 你是中国人，对不对？

   B:

2. *A:*

   B: 对，我喜欢一边吃饭一边看报。

3. *A:* 你很喜欢穿白运动裤，对不对？

   B:

4. *A:*

   B: 不对，台湾的夏天又闷又热。

H. Translate the following into Chinese.

1. You should go to see a doctor right away; otherwise, your cold will become more and more serious. (越来越..., 要不然)

2. I am not going to see the movie because I don't like movies. Besides, I'm too busy. (再说...也)

3. We need to rush to the pharmacy; otherwise, it will be closed. (要不然)

4. My headache is getting worse. (越来越)

5. I am allergic to this kind of medicine. (对)

6. I have seen that movie five times. (次)

7. The doctor examined the patient for a while. (一下)

8. They stood up and walked out of the classroom. (起来, 走出)

9. Mr. Ma is your teacher, isn't he? (对不对)

10. The students are extremely happy today. (死)

Section Two

A. You are sick, and can't go to school. Write a note to your teacher in Chinese. Tell him/her of your problems and how you got these problems.

B. Write about your health history. Please include the following information:
        --When was the last time you visited a doctor, and why?
        --Are you allergic to any medicine?
        --What kind of treatment do you prefer, getting a shot or taking medicine?
        --Do you have any health insurance?

Lesson Seventeen   Dating

I. Listening Comprehension

Section One (Listen to the tape for the textbook) (Multiple choice)

A. Dialogue I (True/False)

(   ) 1. Wang Peng and Li You are in the same Chinese Class.
(   ) 2. Wang Peng likes Li You, but Li You does not like Wang Peng.
(   ) 3. Wang Peng is inviting Li You to see a Chinese movie.
(   ) 4. After the movie, they will go get something to eat.
(   ) 5. They decided not to go to the movie because the tickets are hard to get.
(   ) 6. They will go to the movie with two other friends.

B. Dialogue II (True/False)

(   ) 1. The woman has never seen the man before.
(   ) 2. The man can dance but not the woman.
(   ) 3. The woman does not remember the man at all.
(   ) 4. The man is inviting the woman to a dance.
(   ) 5. The woman is busy this weekend, but she will go out with the man next weekend.
(   ) 6. The woman does chores at home.

Section Two (Listen to the tape for the workbook)

A. Dialogue I (True/False)

(   ) 1. The woman declined the invitation because she was busy.
(   ) 2. The woman is a student, while the man seems to be a librarian.
(   ) 3. The dialogue occurred at 5:30 p.m.
(   ) 4. The man will call the woman in order to help her return her books to the library.

B. Dialogue II (Multiple choice)

(   ) 1. The man was trying to invite Li You _____.
     a. to dinner
     b. to a dancing party
     c. to see a movie

(   ) 2. Li You says she cannot accept the invitation because she has a prior engagement for _____ this evening.
     a. dinner
     b. a concert
     c. a dancing party

(   ) 3. Li You says tomorrow evening she will be _____.
     a. at a restaurant
     b. at a concert
     c. a meeting

II. Speaking Exercises

Section One (Answer the questions in Chinese based on the texts)

A. Dialogue I
1. How did Wang Peng know Li You? Please explain.
2. Do you think that Wang Peng and Li You like each other? Please explain.
3. What will Wang Peng and Li You do this weekend?
4. Do you think that Li You wants to see the Chinese movie? Please explain.
5. Do you think that they will be able to see the movie? Please explain.
6. Who else will be going to the movie with them?

B. Dialogue II
1. How did Bai Jianming meet Li You? Please explain.
2. How did Bai Jianming know Li You's phone number?
3. Can Li You go out with Bai Jianming next weekend after her exam? Please explain.
4. Would Li You be willing to go out with Bai Jianming if she is free? Please explain.

Section Two

A. You met someone at a dance last weekend. You like that person very much. Call that person and invite him/her to have dinner first and then go to a movie. When you make the phone call tell him/her that you danced with him/her last weekend.

B. Someone you don't like is calling you and asking you for a date. Try to decline his/her invitation politely by telling him/her that you will be busy for the next two weekends.

C. Tell your friend that you went to see an excellent opera. The tickets were very difficult to get, but you were able to get the tickets eventually by going through a lot of trouble.

D. Tell a story based on the picture below.

III. Reading Comprehension

Section One (Answer the question about the dialogues)

A. Dialogue I

1. 你觉得李友喜欢王朋吗？为什么？

2. 《活着》的戏票容易买吗？你怎么知道？

3. 李友不想看《活着》，对不对？

4. 一共有几个人一起去看电影？

B. Dialogue II

1. 白健明会跳舞吗？你怎么知道？

2. 白健明为什么打电话给李友？

3. 这几个週末，李友要做什么？

4. 你觉得李友喜欢白健明吗？为什么？

Section Two

A. Read the following passage and answer the questions.(True/False)

> 　　小谢跟小马认识已经快半年了，他们都在同一班学日文。小马去过日本，日文说得比小谢好，所以他常常帮助小谢练习说日文。小马不太会做饭，周末的时候，小谢常常请小马到她家去吃饭，一起说日文，也一起看日文的录像。小马觉得他越来越喜欢小谢。小谢觉得小马是一个很好的人，又聪明，又用功，还很喜欢帮助别的同学。这个星期小谢的爸爸妈妈要来看她，她想把小马介绍给他们。

( )1. 小谢跟小马是同班同学。

( )2. 小谢的日文说得没有小马好。

( )3. 周末的时候, 小谢常常请小马到外头去吃饭。

( )4. 小谢对小马的印象很好。

( )5. 小谢的爸爸妈妈已经见过小马了。

B. Read the following passage and answer the questions.(True/False)

> 　　在中国，很多女孩找对象，喜欢找比自己高，而且年纪比自己大的男孩。以前有的地方同姓的人不能结婚。在台湾，有些男人不喜欢跟比自己小三岁、六岁或者九岁的人结婚，因为很多人说如果这样，结婚以后不会快乐。

( )1. 中国女孩喜欢自己比对象长得高。

( )2. 中国女孩喜欢找年纪比自己小的男孩。

( )3. 以前姓王的不能跟姓王的结婚。

( )4. 台湾男人都不跟比自己小三岁、六岁、或九岁的女人结婚。

IV. Writing and Grammar Exercises

Section One

A. Make sentences using the given phrases.

　　　Example: 玩　高兴

　　　　　===> 昨天我们玩得很高兴。

1. 打球　　　累

2. 跳舞　　　高兴

3. 忙　　　　没有时间睡觉

4. 笑　　　　肚子疼了

5. 看书　　　忘了时间

B. Make "topic-comment" sentences with the given topics.

　　　Example: 学中文：

　　　　　===>学中文，我觉得很有意思。

1. 中文录像：

2. 健康保险：

3. 生日舞会：

4. 住在宿舍里：

5. 在饭馆吃饭：

6. 吃药打针：

C. Complete the following sentences by selecting from the potential complements listed below.

买不到，听不到，吃不到，想不到，想不起来，吃不(习)惯，看不懂，听不懂

1. 她妈妈来美国才半年，_____ 。
    (not used to American food)

2. 我的中文不太好，_____ 。
    (unable to understand Chinese movies)

3. 那个书店只有中文书和英文书，_____ 。
    (unable to buy Japanese books)

4. 老师说话说得太快，_____ 。(unable to understand)

5. 李友的电话号码，_____ 。(unable to recall)

D. Complete the following sentences with 就 .

1. 今天看电影的人真少，_____ 。

2. 我爸爸妈妈说他们要一起开车来看我，_____。

3. 他不会打球，不会唱歌，不会跳舞，_____。

4. 今天来参加小林的生日舞会的人我都不认识，_____。

E. Following the model, combine each pair of the sentences into one.

Example: 我昨天看了一个电影。那个电影很有意思。
===> 我昨天看的那个电影很有意思。

1. 我朋友给我买了一件衣服。那件衣服很合适。

2. 我上个星期天认识了一个朋友。那个朋友很喜欢看歌剧。

3. 我的表姐前天吃了一种药。那种药没有用。

4. 她的男朋友送了她一件衬衫。那件衬衫不便宜。

5. 他的女朋友买了一盘录音带。那盘录音带很好听。

6. 他昨天在图书馆借了一本书。那本书是新的。

F. Translate the time expressions below.

1. next week:

2. the day after tomorrow:

3. the month after next:

4. the week before last:

5. the year after next:

6. the semester after next:

G. Complete the following sentences by using the duplicate forms of the following verbs or verb phrases.

　　庆祝，整理，练习，听录音，打扫房子，打球

1. 功课做完了，_____，你想一起去吗？

2. 老师说我_____，中文就会说得更好。

3. 下个星期六是我妈妈五十岁生日，_____。

4. 今天晚上有很多朋友来我家玩，我得先_____。

5. 我的中文说得还不够好，老师说_____。

6. 你的床上有书，地上也有书，你应该_____。

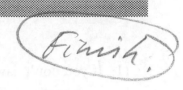

H. Translate the following into Chinese.

1. He finished his homework long time ago. He is watching T.V. now. (早就)

2. I have wanted to watch that video for a long time. (早就)

3. Look at it carefully. It is my book, not yours. (duplication of verb)

4. Forget it. I know you two won't help me. (算了吧，你俩)

5. The day after tomorrow I will go to see an opera with the girl who often helps me.

6. I would like to try it. (reduplication of verb)

7. I am the only one who is going to China to travel. (就)

8. I have not been to New York. (Topic-comment sentence)

9. My father has a very good impression of my boyfriend.

10. He bought too much fruit. We can't eat it all. (complement of potential)

11. If you don't have time to help me clean the house, then forget it. (要是, 就算了)

12. *A:* After the examination, let's have a big celebration. (好好儿, verb duplication)

    B: OK. It's a deal.

Section Two

A. Write a letter to your Chinese friend whom you met last weekend at a birthday party. Tell her/him that you enjoyed dancing with her/him very much, and that you really had a great time at the party. There will be an opera at your school next Friday, and you would like to invite her/him to the opera. Before going to the opera, you would like to have dinner with her/him.

B. Write a couple of paragraphs describing what you did for the past three weekends. You might want to include things such as studying, doing household chores, etc.

Lesson Eighteen   Renting an Apartment

I. Listening Comprehension

Section One (Listen to the tape for the textbook)

A. Narrative (True/False)
(   ) 1. Wang Peng has been living in the dorm for a week so far.
(   ) 2. Wang Peng feels that the dorm is too noisy, and that his room is not big enough.
(   ) 3. It only took Wang Peng two days to find an apartment.
(   ) 4. The apartment is right next to the university. It is very convenient.
(   ) 5. The apartment is furnished, and has its own kitchen too.

B. Dialogue (True/False)
(   ) 1. The apartment is a studio.
(   ) 2. The apartment has a study with a desk and bookcases.
(   ) 3. The rent is $450.00 per month including utilities.
(   ) 4. Pets are not allowed in the apartment.
(   ) 5. Wang Peng decided not to rent the apartment because it is too expensive.

Section Two (Listen to the tape for the workbook)

A. Narrative (True/False)
(   ) 1. In China, all college students live in student dorms.
(   ) 2. All American colleges have student dorms, but not all students live in the dorms.
(   ) 3. Chinese students live in dorms because it is very quiet there.

B. Dialogue (Multiple choice)
(   ) 1. Wang Peng says his apartment is _____.
      a. quiet and convenient but not well furnished
      b. quiet and well furnished but not convenient
      c. quiet and convenient but the kitchen is a bit too small

(   ) 2. It is most likely that tomorrow Wang Peng will eat _____.
      a. in a Chinese restaurant
      b. in his own apartment
      c. in the student dorm where he used to live

(   ) 3. Wang Peng promised to invite the girl _____.
      a. to eat in a restaurant
      b. to a dinner cooked by himself
      c. to cook dinner for him in his apartment

(   ) 4. Which of the following statements can most reasonably be concluded from the dialogue?
      a. Wang Peng is not a good cook yet.
      b. Wang Peng does not want to cook.
      c. The girl is going to teach Wang Peng how to cook.

75

II. Speaking Exercises

Section One (Answer the questions in Chinese based on the texts)

A. Narrative

1. How long has Wang Peng been living in the dorm?
2. Why does Wang Peng wish to move out?
3. How long has Wang Peng been looking for an apartment?
4. How did Wang Peng learn about that apartment?
5. Can you describe that apartment?

B. Dialogue

1. How did Wang Peng start his phone call to the landlord? How did the landlord respond to him?
2. What did the landlord say about the furniture in that apartment?
3. What is the $450.00 for? Please explain.
4. Can you keep your dog in the apartment? Why?

Section Two

A. Describe the place you live in Chinese. Don't forget to mention the furniture!

B. You don't like the house you are currently living in, so you are making phone calls to look for a new one. Ask about the rent, environment, and facilities.

C. Tell a story based on the picture below.

III. Reading Comprehension

Section One (Answer the questions about the dialogues)

A. Narrative

1. 王朋现在住在哪儿？住了多久了？

2. 王朋为什么要找公寓？

3. 王朋怎么找公寓？

4. 王朋觉得那套公寓方便吗？合适吗？为什么？

B. Dialogue II

1. 那套公寓有几个卧室？

2. 那套公寓有什么家具？

3. 王朋是不是一个很吵的人？你怎么知道？

4. 如果你要租那套公寓，你得付四百五十元押金，对不对？

5. 你可以在公寓养狗吗？为什么？

Section Two

A. Read the following passage and answer the questions. (True/False)

> 小马现在住在学生宿舍，他一个人住一个房间。宿舍里有餐厅、图书室、电脑室，还有洗衣房，非常方便。小马不太会做饭，很喜欢认识新朋友，所以他很喜欢住宿舍。他听说在校外租房子比住宿舍便宜，但是得跟别人一起住，还得自己做饭。小马虽然想住便宜的房子，但是不想自己做饭，所以他现在还不知道他下学期是不是应该搬出去住。

( )1. 小马有自己的房间。
( )2. 小马不喜欢住宿舍。
( )3. 小马觉得在餐厅吃饭很方便。
( )4. 在校外租房子比住学校宿舍便宜。
( )5. 小马下学期要搬到校外去住。

B. Read the following passage and answer the questions.(True/False)

> 在台湾租房子要付一个月的房租当押金。以后要是想搬走，必须在搬家前一个月让房东知道，要不然押金就拿不回来了。另外，搬家的时候也得把房子打扫干净。

( )1. 在台湾租房子得付押金。
( )2. 在台湾租房子一次得住一年，要不然押金就拿不回来。
( )3. 搬家的时候房东会帮你打扫房子。

IV. Writing and Grammar Exercises

Section One

A. Complete the following short dialogues.

1. *A:* 你听录音听了几个钟头了？

   B: _____ 。

2. *A:* _____ 。

   B: 我学中文学了八个月了。

3. *A:* 你上大学上了多久了？

   B: _____ 。

B. Rewrite the following sentences using the structure "连...都/也..."

1. 他忘了女朋友的生日。

2. 我最近很忙，没有时间睡觉。

3. 他中文学得很好，看得懂中文小说。

4. 这个房间很小，放不下一张书桌。

5. 这个字很难，老师不会写。

C. Follow the model, and rewrite the following sentences using the structure "question word + 都."

　　　　Example: *A:* 他常常看录像吗？

　　　　　　　　B: 他什么录像都不看。

1. *A:* 你的朋友会唱什么歌？

   B: _____ 。

2. A: 除了听音乐以外，今天晚上你还想做什么？

   B: _____ 。

3. A: 这个孩子喜欢看什么书？

   B: _____ 。

4. A: 你饿了吧，想吃什么？

   B: 我肚子疼，_____ 。

D. Complete the following dialogue.

   A: 你在这个公寓住了多久了？(more than a year)

   B:

   A: 房租每个月多少钱？(six hundred)

   B:

   A: 押金多少钱？(one thousand)

   B:

   A: 你可以在你的公寓里养动物吗？(not allowed)

   B:

   A: 你的公寓带家具吗？(not furnished)

   B:

   A: 要是你想找一个可以养动物和带家具的公寓，我可以帮你看报上的广告。
      (No, thanks. I can read the newspaper myself.)

   B:

E. Translate the following into Chinese.

1. He has slept for over twenty hours (but less than 30). (V+了+Nu+M+Time+了，多)

2. How can we study Lesson Ten when we haven't studied Lesson Nine yet? （连...都，怎么）

3. He didn't like any of the apartments. (interrogative pronoun with 都)

4. He reads all kinds of advertisements. (什么...都)

5. I have a little over ten dollars (less than eleven).

6. You'd better not rent that apartment because it is not furnished. (最好)

7. There is a sofa in the living room. In addition, there are a bookshelf and a desk in the living room. (有，还有)

8. There are two single beds in the bedroom. One is on the left side, and the other is on the right side. (有)

9. The kitchen is too small. There is no room for a dining table and six chairs. (V＋不下)

10. Yesterday evening, over twenty people went to see the movie. (多)

11. My apartment is only one mile away from the school. (离)

12. No pets are allowed in this dormitory. (interrogative pronoun with 都, 许)

Section Two

A. Write a letter to your friend asking him/her to find you a one-bedroom apartment near the university. You prefer a furnished apartment under $500.00 per month. You don't mind paying a security deposit, but you do not wish to pay for utilities. Also, since you have a dog, you need to find a place where pets are allowed.

B. You wish to rent out the extra room in your house. Can you write an advertisement for it? Be sure to include the following information:
  -- The room is furnished with a single bed, a desk, two chairs, and two bookshelves
  -- Utilities are included
  -- One month rent required for security deposit
  -- Monthly rent is $250.00
  -- Quiet people preferred

Lesson Nineteen   Post Office

I. Listening Comprehension

Section One (Listen to the tape for the textbook)

A. Dialogue I (True/False)
(   ) 1. The woman wished to mail a letter to Tainan.
(   ) 2. The woman decided to send the letter by express mail.
(   ) 3. The postage for the express mail was fourteen dollars.
(   ) 4. In addition to mailing the letter, the woman also bought some stamps.
(   ) 5. A postcard costs three dollars.

B. Dialogue II (True/False)
(   ) 1. The man is seeking advice from the woman.
(   ) 2. The man used to send flowers to Zhang Yiwen on her birthday.
(   ) 3. Zhang Yiwen and the man live in the same city.
(   ) 4. The man deposited the check into the bank.

Section Two (Listen to the tape for the workbook)

A. Dialogue (Multiple choice)
(   ) 1. How many days does it usually take for a letter to travel from here to New York?
    a. At least three days.
    b. At least five days.
    c. At least a week.

(   ) 2. Based on the dialogue, which of the following statements is true?
    a. If the man's brother sends him a letter from New York, his brother will get his reply at least two weeks later.
    b. If the man's brother writes to somebody in New York, he will get the reply at least seven days later.
    c. If the man writes to his brother in New York, he will get his reply after six or seven days at the earliest.

(   ) 3. Judging from the context, the word "huíxìn" means _____.
    a. a letter returned to the sender
    b. a letter sent in reply
    c. a letter to one's relative

(   ) 4. Last Monday the man wrote a letter to _____.
    a. himself for fun
    b. the postmaster
    c. his brother

(   ) 5. Last Wednesday the man received a letter written by _____.
     a. himself
     b. his brother
     c. the postmaster

B. Narrative (True/False)
(   ) 1. According to the passage, Wang Peng did not have a credit card when he was in China.
(   ) 2. Wang Peng heard from his friends that many people in China and Taiwan are starting to use credit cards.
(   ) 3. Wang Peng uses his credit card only in restaurants.

II. Speaking Exercises

Section One (Answer the questions in Chinese based on the dialogues)

A. Dialogue I
1. How long does it take to send a letter from Taipei to Tainan by regular mail? How about express mail?
2. Is the woman sending the letter by regular mail or express mail? Why?
3. How much extra will it cost if the woman wants to send the letter by registered mail?
4. Did the woman buy anything else besides the stamps?
5. What is the $141.00 dollars for? Please explain.

B. Dialogue II
1. What did the man give Zhang Yiwen for her birthday in the past?
2. What did the woman suggest that the man buy for Zhang Yiwen's birthday? Why?
3. How will the man have the present delivered to Zhang Yiwen?
4. Who sent the man a check? Can he deposit it in the post office?
5. What currency does the post office accept?

Section Two

A. You are in a post office in Taiwan and would like to send a very important letter to your parents in New York. Find out how many days it takes to send an air mail letter to New York, and how much the postage costs. Also find out how much extra you need to pay if you want to send the letter by registered mail.

B. You go to a post office in Beijing to buy stamps and send something, but you run into some problems. Ask the clerk to help you.

III. Reading Exercises

Section I

A. Dialogue I

1. 留学生现在在哪儿？她要寄信到哪儿？

2. 寄平信要几天？寄快信呢？

3. 为什么留学生要寄挂号快信？

4. 她寄一封挂号快信一共要多少钱？

5. 除了寄信以外，留学生在邮局还买别的东西了吗？

6. 留学生花了多少钱买明信片？

7. 十张邮票要多少钱？

B. Dialogue II

1. 下个月是谁的生日？

2. 白先生以前送过花给张意文吗？你怎么知道？

3. 白先生住在上海吗？你怎么知道？

4. 从北京可以送花到上海吗？怎么送？

5. 白先生把一张美金支票存在邮局里，对不对？为什么？

Section Two

A. Read the passage below and answer the questions. (True/False)

小张从中国来美国念书已经半年了，他很想念他在北京的家人，一个星期写一封信回家。他很想跟家里的人聊天，可是电话费太贵，每分钟要一块多，所以他一个半月才往家里打一次电话。每次打电话，爸爸妈妈都不让他说得太久，因为不想让他花太多钱。

( )1. 小张是中国人。
( )2. 小张一个月写四封信回家。
( )3. 从来美国到现在，小张已经往家里打过十二次电话了。
( )4. 因为不常打电话，小张每次打电话都跟家里的人聊很久。

B. Read the passage below and answer the questions. (True/False)

以前小马出去旅行的时候，不买旅行支票，也没有信用卡，所以他带很多现金。有一次，他到日本去玩，离开美国以前，到银行去拿了两千块美金的现金。到东京的第二天，他的钱就丢了。他在日本因为没有钱，所以玩得一点都不高兴。小马想以后出门，一定要买旅行支票，现金只带一点就可以了。

( )1. 小马以前出去旅行用旅行支票。
( )2. 他去日本以前，在美国换了一些日元。
( )3. 他丢的钱，很快就找到了。
( )4. 小马以后到别的地方旅行，不会带很多现金。

IV. Writing and Grammar Exercises

Section One

A. Answer the following questions.

1. *A:* 从学校寄信到你家要多少天？

   B: _____ 。

2. *A:* 从纽约开车到你家要多久？

   B: _____ 。

3. *A:* 从你的宿舍到图书馆远不远？怎么走？

   B: _____ 。

4. *A:* 从开始学中文到现在，你学了多少汉字了？

   B: _____ 。

B. Complete the following short conversations:

1. *A:* 一张明信片_____ ？我想买五张。

   B: _____ 两块钱，五张一共 _____ 。

2. *A:* 除了五张明信片，我还要买十张邮票，一张 _____ ？

   B: _____ 三块钱。

3. *A:* _____ ？

   B: _____ 十块钱，十张_____ 。

      一共 _____ 。

C. Answer the following questions with approximate numerals.
    Example: 你多久去一次图书馆？

    ===>我每两、三天去一次图书馆。

1. 你多久给你妈妈打一次电话？

2. 你们常常几个人一起出去吃饭？

3. 十九岁的学生可能上大学几年级？

4. 你一个月花多少钱？

D. Following the model, rewrite the following sentences using the expression
   "除了...都".
    Example: 今天晚上我只想看报，不想做别的事。

    ===> 今天晚上除了看报以外，别的事我都不想做。

1. 我只喝茶，不喝别的。

2. 住宿舍我就怕吵，别的都不怕。

3. 只有一个同学没预习课文，别的同学都预习了。

4. 我们都去过北京，可是我弟弟还没有去过北京。

E. Fill in the blanks with 还 or 都 .

1. 你周末除了跳舞以外，＿＿＿＿＿＿喜欢做什么？

2. 除了小张以外，我们＿＿＿＿＿＿不吃牛肉。

3. 老王除了报纸以外，什么＿＿＿＿＿＿不看。

4. 我的房间里除了一张床以外，什么＿＿＿＿＿＿没有。

5. 除了书桌以外，她＿＿＿＿＿＿买了两个书架。

6. 除了首饰以外，他＿＿＿＿＿＿常常给女朋友送花。

F. Complete the following sentences with 越...越... .
　　　　Example: 我觉得房子越大越好。 (the bigger the better)

1. 他很喜欢买衣服，他告诉我＿＿＿＿＿＿＿＿＿＿＿＿＿＿＿＿＿＿＿＿＿＿。
   (the more the better)

2. 学生都说考试＿＿＿＿＿＿＿＿＿＿＿＿＿＿＿＿＿＿＿＿＿＿＿＿＿＿＿。
   (the easier the better)

3. 这种水果＿＿＿＿＿＿＿＿＿＿＿＿＿＿＿＿＿＿＿＿＿＿＿＿＿＿＿＿＿＿。
   (the bigger the tastier)

4. 这种首饰＿＿＿＿＿＿＿＿＿＿＿＿＿＿＿＿＿＿＿＿＿＿＿＿＿＿＿＿＿＿。
   (the smaller the more expensive)

G. Translate the following into Chinese:

1. How long does it take to send a letter by regular mail from Beijing to New York?
   （从...到）

2. I'd like to buy five bottles of fruit juice. How much for each? (一. . . 多少钱)

3. It's one dollar and twenty cents for each bottle. Altogether it's six dollars. (一共)

4. This kind of pants is very expensive. They cost fifty or sixty dollars a pair. (approximate numerals)

5. The more money a bank has, the better. (越. . . 越. . .)

6. I can do everything except cook. (除了. . . 以外，都)

7. In addition to playing the piano, I also like to travel and play ball. (除了. . . 还)

8. She has been driving faster and faster recently. (越. . . 越. . .)

9. My father said that I cannot go traveling in China unless I learn Chinese well first. (先. . . 才)

10. The teacher asks us to listen to the tapes two or three hours everyday. (approximate numerals)

11. Her boyfriend gave her a bunch of flowers as her birthday present. (当)

12. If I send by express mail, when can my friend receive this letter?

Section Two

A. Write a letter to your friend in Taiwan to find out how the post office works there.
Ask him/her the cost for the following:
-- Sending a letter by regular mail from one city to another in Taiwan.
-- Sending a letter by air mail from Taiwan to the United States.
-- A postcard.
-- Sending a letter by registered mail from one city to another city in Taiwan.

B. Write a letter to your Chinese friend explaining that it normally takes 2 to 3 days to send a letter from New York to Boston. If you want the letter to get there as soon as possible, you should send it through express mail which only takes one day. Also, tell your friend that while one can deposit money at the post office in China, one cannot do it in the United States. Neither do post offices in the United States sell postcards.

Lesson Twenty   Sports

I. Listening Comprehension

Section One (Listen to the tape for the textbook)

A. Dialogue I (True/False)

(   ) 1. The man eats a lot, but he also exercises a lot.
(   ) 2. The woman suggests that the man exercise at least three hours each week.
(   ) 3. The man did not jog in the past two years.
(   ) 4. The man prefers to jog in the winter rather than in the summer.
(   ) 5. The man thinks that playing basketball is a lot of trouble.
(   ) 6. The man likes to swim because he can do it by himself.

B. Dialogue II (True/False)

(   ) 1. Siwen came to the States to go to college.
(   ) 2. Siwen watches TV every day because he wants to improve his English.
(   ) 3. The woman likes to watch football.
(   ) 4. They are watching a soccer match on the TV.

Section Two (Listen to the tape for the workbook)

A. Dialogue (Multiple choice)

(   ) 1. What sports are mentioned in the dialogue?
        a. Basketball, football, and swimming.
        b. Football, tennis, and swimming.
        c. Basketball, tennis, and swimming.
        d. Football, swimming, and table tennis.

(   ) 2. Why did the man quit playing tennis?
        a. It is too hot to play tennis in the summer.
        b. He feels very tired after playing it.
        c. It is too costly for him.
        d. He thinks that tennis is not as exciting as basketball.

(   ) 3. Which of the statements is most likely to be true?
        a. The man loves several kinds of sports.
        b. The man loves basketball more than swimming.
        c. The man has failed to persevere in any of the sports.
        d. The man hates basketball but loves tennis.

(   ) 4. What sport (or sports) is the man engaged in right now?
        a. Swimming   b. No sport at all
        c. Football   d. Tennis and basketball

B. Narrative (True/False)

(   ) 1. Wang Peng started to like American football as soon as he came to the U.S.

(   ) 2. Wang Peng used to think that American football was too dangerous.

(   ) 3. Wang Peng likes basketball better than American football.

(   ) 4. Wang Peng never watches American football games on TV.

II. Speaking Exercises

Section One (Answer the questions in Chinese based on the dialogues)

A. Dialogue I

1. What did the man say about his body?

2. How did the woman respond to the man?

3. What did the woman suggest the man do to lose weight?

4. What sport did the man decide to do?

B. Dialogue II

1. Who is Siwen? Why did Siwen come to the States?

2. Why does Siwen watch TV for two hours every day?

3. What is playing on channel 6?

4. Does the man like to watch football? Please explain.

5. Why did the woman tell the man not to worry about the football players?

Section Two

A. Among the sports listed below, which one do you like the most? Which one do you like the least? Why?

   --Tennis, basketball, soccer, jogging, swimming, football, etc.

B. Explain to your Chinese friend the differences between soccer and football.

C. Describe the two sports below. Do point out their differences.

A   B

III. Reading Exercises

Section I

A. Dialogue I

1. 为什么老李的肚子越来越大？

2. 小林说肚子怎么可以小一点儿？

3. 老李为什么说跑步很难受？

4. 老李为什么不想打网球？

5. 老李为什么说打篮球很麻烦？

6. 老李喜欢游泳吗？为什么？

7. 你想老李会更胖吗？为什么？

B. Dialogue II

1. 思文来美国做什么？

2. 思文为什么每天看电视？

3. 思文喜欢看美式足球吗？你是怎么知道的？

4. 国际足球跟美式足球有什么不同？

5. 思文喜欢看美式足球赛吗？你是怎么知道的？

Section Two

A. Read the passage below and answer the questions. (True/False)

台湾人很喜欢看棒球比赛，因为十几年前台湾的棒球队打得很好，常常得世界冠军。那个时候常常在美国比赛，因为美国跟台湾有十几个小时的时差，所以为了看球赛，台湾人常常半夜起来看电视。

( ) 1. 台湾的棒球队没有得过世界冠军。
( ) 2. 美国是白天的时候，台湾是晚上。
( ) 3. 以前台湾人看棒球赛的时候，连觉都可以不睡。

B. Read the passage below and answer the questions. (True/False)

中国的年轻人跟老年人都喜欢运动。很多年轻人不但喜欢打乒乓球，而且打得很好。打乒乓球跟打篮球不一样，个子不必太高，所以是一种很适合中国人的运动。中国的老年人喜欢早上到公园去打太极拳，打完太极拳以后，他们常常先跟朋友聊一会天儿再回家。

( ) 1. 中国很多的年轻人很会打乒乓球。
( ) 2. 打乒乓球的人个子越高越好。
( ) 3. 每天早上公园里有很多老年人在打太极拳。
( ) 4. 老年人打完太极拳以后，马上回家。

IV. Writing and Grammar Exercises

Section One

A. Complete the following sentences using the negative forms.

Example: 我饿死了，<u>已经（有）两天没吃饭了</u>。
   (have not eaten for two days)

1. 王朋去哪儿了？_____。
   (have not seen him for two weeks)

2. *A:* 你学过日文吗？

   B: 学过，学过三年。

   A: 你可以教我吗？

   B: 不行，_____，已经忘了。

      (have not spoken Japanese for a long time)

3. 小白忙极了，_____。

   (has not called his mother for two months)

4. 小张很想去中国饭馆，因为_____。

   (has not eaten Chinese food for half a year)

5. 他的身体越来越不好，因为_____。

   (has not exercised for more than a year)

B. Fill in the blanks with "住下去, 说下去, 热下去, 跳下去, 学下去."

1. 天气太热了，真受不了，再_____，我就要热死了。

2. 这个宿舍太吵，我不想_____了。

3. 虽然中文很难，但是我还是想_____。

4. 你唱歌唱得太难听了，别_____了。

5. 我跳舞已经跳了五个小时了，再_____，就要累死了。

C. Rewrite the following sentences using "起來."

Example: 她一回家就开始听录音。

===>她一回家就听起录音来。

1. 他刚上课，头就开始疼了。

2. 现在才三月，天气就开始热了。

3. 他吃得很多，又不运动，开始胖了。

4. 他们一考完试，就开始打球。

D. Answer the following questions using "被."

Example: A: 请问，你们这间房子出租吗？(rented by someone, 租)

B: 对不起，<u>房子已经被人租去了</u>。

1. A: 你可以把新买的书借我看看吗？(borrowed by someone, 借)

B: 对不起，_____。

2. A: 我的网球拍怎么坏了？(ruined by younger brother, 打)

B: 你的网球拍_____。

3. A: 妈妈，再给我一些钱吧。(taken away by older brother, 拿)

B: 我昨天刚给你两百块，你都花了？

A: 没有，_____。

4. A: 你的手怎么了？(crushed, 压)

B: 我的手受伤了，是昨天足球比赛的时候_____。

D. Fill in the blanks with "起來" and "下去."

　　昨天下午我在学校看到我的小学同学老田，我们聊了＿＿＿＿＿＿。我看他比以前瘦了，就问他为什么。他告诉我，他以前不太忙，很舒服，可是最近开始考试了，所以忙＿＿＿＿＿了。我告诉他，他不能再瘦＿＿＿＿＿了，要多注意自己的身体健康。他说，他在宿舍住很不习惯。我说，住宿舍对学英文有好处，你还是住＿＿＿＿＿吧，几个月以后你的英文就会好＿＿＿＿＿＿了。

E. Answer the following questions.

1. 你多长时间看一次电影？

2. 你多长时间运动一次？每次运动多久？

3. 你多长时间去一次中国饭馆？

4. 你多长时间上一次银行？

5. 你多久没看到你的爸爸了？

6. 你多久没打电话给你的好朋友了？

7. 你多久没看电视了？

8. 你多久没写信了？

F. Translate the following into Chinese.

1. I haven't been to school for a week. (没...了)

2. My younger brother has bought three tennis rackets so far this year. (了...了)

3. As soon as he finished his meal, he started to watch TV. (一...就, 起来)

4. Please stop saying that. I find it hard to bear. (下去, 难受)

5. I have not had a bath for three days. It's very uncomfortable. (duration + 了)

6. I have been playing tennis for more than ten years. (duration + 了)

7. She jogs 40 minutes everyday. (duration)

8. Many football players have been hurt by being crushed. (被)

9. In order to improve his listening comprehension, he listens to recordings two hours a day. (为了)

10. I don't like to watch (American) football because I can't tell who is winning and who is losing.

Section Two

A. Describe the exercises that you do to stay fit. How often do you exercise? And for how long each time?

B. Write a letter to your Chinese friend telling him/her what sports are popular in the States. Describe your personal feelings toward those sports.

Lesson Twenty-One   Travel

I. Listening Comprehension

Section One (Listen to the tape for the textbook)

A. Dialogue I (True/False)

(   ) 1. The woman is going to Taiwan in one month.
(   ) 2. The man has never been to Taiwan before.
(   ) 3. The man will leave for Taiwan in the middle of June.
(   ) 4. The man has already purchased the plane ticket.
(   ) 5. Both Northwest Airlines and China Airlines are having a sale.

B. Dialogue II (Multiple choice)

(   ) 1. What does the man want to buy?
        a. A one-way ticket to Beijing.
        b. A round-trip ticket to Beijing.
        c. A one way ticket to Washington, D.C.
        d. A round-trip ticket to Washington, D.C.
(   ) 2. Where does the man's trip begin?
        a. Beijing.
        b. Washington, D.C.
        c. Chicago.
        d. Los Angeles.
(   ) 3. Where will the man spend a night during his trip?
        a. Chicago.
        b. Los Angeles.
        c. Seoul.
        d. Hong Kong.
(   ) 4. What airline has the lowest fare?
        a. Air China.
        b. Northwest Airlines.
        c. Korean Airlines.
        d. US Air.
(   ) 5. What will happen next week?
        a. There will be a sale.
        b. The price will go up.
        c. The ticket will be issued.
        d. The deposit will be returned.

Section Two (Listen to the tape for the workbook)

A. Dialogue (Multiple choice)

(   ) 1. If you fly round trip with Northwest Airlines from New York to Beijing, how
        much will it cost you, according to the dialogue?
        a. $1,020   b. $1,200   c. $1,380   d. $1,400

(   ) 2. Why didn't the man want to fly Korean Airlines? Because of the _____.
         a. price   b. aircraft   c. connection   d. service
(   ) 3. How long did the man plan to stay in Beijing?
         a. one week   b. two weeks   c. three weeks   d. one month
(   ) 4. Why did the man decide not to order the ticket in the end?
         a. He had no credit card.
         b. He did not want to give his credit card number.
         c. He did not want to write a check.
         d. He had not got his visa yet.

B. Narrative (True/False)
(   ) 1. Little Gao went to Chicago for a visit two years ago, but has never been to New
          York.
(   ) 2. Little Gao plans to go to New York two or three weeks after the semester ends.
(   ) 3. According to the passage, the price of the airline ticket is at least twice as much
          as that of the bus ticket.
(   ) 4. According to the passage, it takes about an hour to get a bus ticket but twenty-
          four hours to get a plane ticket.

II. Speaking Exercises

Section One (Answer the questions in Chinese based on the dialogues)

A. Dialogue I
1. What does the man intend to do in Taiwan?
2. What advice did the woman give to the man concerning his trip to Taiwan?
3. Did the man have any idea about buying airline tickets? Has he bought a ticket yet?
4. Why did the woman say that her brother can help the man?

B. Dialogue II
1. Why did the man call the travel agency?
2. How much is a round-trip ticket to Beijing?
3. What airline does the man prefer?
4. What will the man's itinerary be if he flies Korean Airlines to Beijing?
5. What did the woman say when the man asked her about direct flight to Beijing?
6. What is the final advice that the woman gave to the man?

Section Two

A. Situational Conversation: Find a partner to be your travel agent. You call the agent
    to book a plane ticket. You are going to Taipei at the end of August. You would like
    to leave on a Monday and return on a Saturday. Select the best flight based on price
    and dates. Your partner will try to be as helpful as possible.

B. Talk about your most enjoyable trip or the most recent one.

III. Reading Exercises

Section One

A. Dialogue I

1. 放假的时候小白打算到哪里去？

2. 小钱计划到台湾去做什么？

3. 小钱什么时候要到台湾去？

4. 去台湾以前，小钱得做哪些事？

5. 昨天小钱看报了吗？你怎么知道？

6. 为什么小白要小钱把他的旅行日程告诉他？

7. 为什么小白要小钱请他吃饭？

B. Dialogue II

1. 王朋给哪家旅行社打电话？

2. 王朋为什么给旅行社打电话？

3. 王朋想买哪家航空公司的机票？

4. 要是王朋坐韩航的飞机，得在什么地方住一个晚上？

5. 哪几家航空公司有从洛杉矶直飞北京的班机？

6. 为什么旅行社的职员要王朋早一点订票？

7. 西北航空公司的机票最便宜，对不对？

Section Two

A. Read the passage below and answer the questions. (True/False)

台北有很多美国人，他们有的是到台湾去旅行，有的是去学中文，有的是去教英文。也有很多人一边教英文，一边学中文，有空的时候就到各地去旅行。几年前，台北有很多人想跟美国人学英文，所以教英文的工作不太难找。可是现在那里的外国人越来越多，所以教英文的工作越来越难找了。还有外国人必须有工作证才能在台湾工作，要不然是不合法的。

( ) 1. 在台北的美国人都有工作。

( ) 2. 有的美国人到台湾只想去旅行。

( ) 3. 有很多台北人想跟美国人学英文。

( ) 4. 现在外国人在台北找教英文的工作不太难。

( ) 5. 外国人要有工作证才可以在台湾教英文。

B. Read the passage below and answer the questions. (True/False)

小白在加州大学念书，放假的时候他常常跟朋友到各地去玩。因为坐飞机太贵，所以他很少坐飞机。他最喜欢开车到各州的国家公园去看看，有的国家公园，他已经去过两、三次了。出去旅行的时候他很少住旅馆，多半是在公园露营，因为只要付一点钱，就可以在露营的地方住，那里也有洗澡间和厕所，很便宜。每次出去玩，他都租车，因为他的车是旧车，不太适合长途旅行。而且租的车要是有了问题，可以打电话请租车公司来换车，比开自己的车方便得多。

( ) 1. 小白在加州上学。

( ) 2. 小白放假的时候喜欢一个人去旅行。

( ) 3. 小白旅行的时候常常坐飞机。

( ) 4. 小白旅行的时候不常住旅馆，常常露营。

( ) 5. 在公园露营不必付钱。

( ) 6. 露营的地方可以洗澡、上厕所。

（　）7. 小白的车不是新车。

（　）8. 小白有时候开自己的车去旅行。

（　）9. 旅行的时候，租车比开自己的车方便。

IV. Writing and Grammar Exercises

Section One

A. Translate the following into Chinese.

1. to give a discount:

2. 20% off :

3. 15% off:

4. half price:

B.   Following the model, rewrite the sentences using the expression "有的. . . 有的. "

　　　Example:在我家，爸爸和弟弟喜欢吃中国饭，妈妈和妹妹喜欢吃美国饭。

　　　===> 在我家，有的人喜欢吃中国饭，有的人喜欢吃美国饭。

1. 在运动场上，有很多人在打球，还有一些人在跑步。

2. 韩国航空公司和中国民航的机票很便宜，西北航空公司的机票很贵。

3. 来美国的中国人，有很多人是来念书的，也有一些人是来工作的。

4. 在图书馆裏，很多人在看书，也有一些人在看报。

5. 周末，我常常出去打球，也常常去看电影。

C. Following the model, answer the questions using interrogative pronouns.

　　Example: *A:* 你想租哪个房子？(whichever is cheap)

　　　　　　B: 哪个房子便宜，我就租哪个。

1. *A:* 你姐姐喜欢买什麼衣服？(whatever is expensive)

　　B: ＿＿＿＿＿＿＿＿＿＿＿＿＿＿＿＿＿ 。

2. *A:* 你想住哪个公寓？(whichever is the nearest to the school)

　　B: ＿＿＿＿＿＿＿＿＿＿＿＿＿＿＿＿＿ 。

3. *A:* 你想看什么电影？(whatever is interesting)

　　B: ＿＿＿＿＿＿＿＿＿＿＿＿＿＿＿＿＿ 。

4. *A:* 我们去哪家饭馆？(whichever is good)

　　B: ＿＿＿＿＿＿＿＿＿＿＿＿＿＿＿＿＿ 。

D. Following the model, make sentences using the pattern "先...然后."

　　Example: 复习　　　考试

　　　===>你应该先复习，然后去考试。

1. 问票价　　　　　买机票

2. 预习　　　　　　上课

3. 看医生　　吃药

4. 吃饭   付钱

5. 去图书馆   去活动中心

E. Following the model, describe your itinerary.

     Example: 北京 - - - >香港 - - - >洛杉矶 - - - >纽约

     ===> 先从北京飞到香港，在香港转机，再从香港飞到洛杉矶，
         然后从洛杉矶飞到纽约。

1. 香港 - - - >东京 - - - >芝加哥 - - - >纽约

2. 华盛顿 - - - >芝加哥 - - - >洛杉矶 - - - >台北

3. 波士顿 - - - >东京 - - - >上海 - - - >北京

F. Following the model, make questions and answer them.

      Example: 这条蓝裤子十八块钱，那条黄裤子二十块。

      ===> *A*:黄裤子比蓝裤子贵多少？

              B:黄裤子比蓝裤子贵两块。

1. 从芝加哥到香港，西北航空公司的票价是一千一百五十块，
   韩航是一千一百块。

    A: _____ 。

    B: _____ 。

2. 这个大电脑一千块钱，那个小电脑两千多块。

    A: _____ 。

    B: _____ 。

3. 现在订机票三百五十块一张，一个星期以後五百三十块一张。

    A: _____ 。

    B: _____ 。

4. 我只有一个网球拍，可是我的弟弟有五个。

    A: _____ 。

    B: _____ 。

5. 中国民航的飞机早上八点离开北京，西北航空公司的是下午一点离开北京。

    A: _____ 。

    B: _____ 。

G. Write the following numbers in Chinese characters.

1. 50,000:

2. 98,764:

3. 30,607:

4. 708,050:

5. 123,456:

6. 6,700,000:

7. 4,000,398:

8. 26,505,489:

9. 700,400,300:

10. 4,386,509,712:

H. Translate the following into Chinese.

1. All bookshelves are on sale, but some are 20% off while others are 30% off. (打折扣, 有的...有的...)

2. I often get sick. Sometimes I have a stomachache, and sometimes I have a headache. (有的...有的...)

3. We will go to whichever travel agency is good. (哪...哪...)

4. We will have dinner first and then go to a movie. After that we will go dancing. (先...再...然后)

5. The hot-and-sour soup in this restaurant tastes better than that in the other restaurant. And it is also cheaper than the other. (比)

6. He hopes he can take a trip to China in two years. (内)

7. If you pay me now, you can get the plane ticket tomorrow. (要是/ 如果...就...)

8. I want to go to whichever bank you go to. (哪. . .哪. . .)

9. I say whatever I want to. Whoever wants to listen can listen. I am not worried.
    （什么. . .什么; 谁. . .谁）

10. Hurry up. You have to come back in an hour. (内)

11. I heard that it is very difficult to get a visa for the month of August. You'd
    better apply for one right away. (最好)

12. The advertisement says that Northwest Airlines tickets are 25% off. (打. . 折)

13. If you send by express mail, it will be there in two days. (要是/ 如果. . 就)

14. Call me if the passport is done. (要是/ 如果. . 就)

Section Two

A. School is almost over. Please write a paragraph describing your ideal travel plan for a two-month summer vacation. Where would you go? Who would you go with? What would you do? How would you travel?

B. Write a letter to your travel agency and ask them to reserve a plane ticket for you
    when the tickets are on sale next time. You plan to make a trip from Washington,
    D.C. to Shanghai. If possible, you would like to fly directly from Washington, D.C. to
    China because you don't like to change planes. Also, tell them that you will fly the
    airline which offers the lowest fare.

Lesson Twenty-Two   Hometown

I. Listening Comprehension

Section One (Listen to the tape for the textbook)

A. Dialogue I (True/False)
(   ) 1. The man is going to California during the spring break.
(   ) 2. The woman is going to visit her grandparents during the spring break.
(   ) 3. The man has no relatives in the United States.
(   ) 4. The man's aunt lives in San Francisco.
(   ) 5. The woman is from a big city.
(   ) 6. The man has been to the woman's hometown.

B. Dialogue II (True/False)
(   ) 1. The man has lived in the States for more than a year.
(   ) 2. The man is homesick.
(   ) 3. The man's hometown is a political center.
(   ) 4. The man's hometown has four distinctive seasons.
(   ) 5. The man intends to go home during his winter break.

Section Two (Listen to the tape for the workbook)

A. Dialogue (Multiple choice)
(   ) 1. Which of the following is the most reasonable estimate of the distance from Wang Peng's hometown to Beijing?
    a. 2 miles   b. 200 miles   c. 50 miles   d. 500 miles

(   ) 2. Wang Peng left his hometown_____ ago.
    a. over two years
    b. exactly two years
    c. about three years
    d. twenty months

(   ) 3. Which of the following statements is most likely to be true?
    a. Wang Peng and his friends used to swim in the river.
    b. Li You once swam in the river near Wang Peng's hometown.
    c. Wang Peng and Li You once swam in the river near Wang Peng's hometown.
    d. Wang Peng used to swim in the river alone.

(   ) 4. According to the dialogue, what does Li You think of Wang Peng's hometown?
    a. She thinks it is too close to Beijing.
    b. She loves it and hopes to visit it.
    c. She hopes there will be a swimming pool there.
    d. She thinks it is too far away from the United States.

B. Narrative (True/False)

(   ) 1. According to the passage, Los Angeles is a relatively quiet city in spite of the busy traffic.

(   ) 2. Because there are too many vehicles and pedestrians on the streets, life in Los Angeles is not convenient.

(   ) 3. People complain that the weather in Los Angeles is not good because it seldom rains and almost never snows.

(   ) 4. Little Gao's aunt loves Los Angeles and refuses to move away from it.

(   ) 5. Little Gao's aunt loves skiing and would not be bothered too much by cold weather.

II. Speaking Exercises

Section One (Answer the questions in Chinese based on the dialogues)

A. Dialogue I

1. Who is Wang Dezhong? Where does he live? What is he discussing with Li You?
2. What does Li You intend to do during her spring break? How about Wang Dezhong?
3. Could you tell me something about Wang Dezhang's grandparents, his aunt and his uncle?
4. How did Li You describe her hometown?
5. What can you do in Li You's hometown in the four different seasons?

B. Dialogue II

1. How long has Wang Peng been living in the United States?
2. Does Wang Peng like the United States? Please explain.
3. Is Beijing an important city? Why?
4. How did Wang Peng describe Beijing's weather?
5. Why did the woman say that Wang Peng could be the tour guide?

Section Two

A. Describe the geographical settings and climate of your hometown.

B. Talk about your relatives, including what they do and where they live, etc.

C. Describe this picture using what you have learned so far.

III. Reading Exercises

Section One

A. Dialogue I

1. 王德中住在什么地方？

2. 王德中有什么亲戚住在加州？

3. 李友的老家在旧金山，对不对？

4. 李友老家在一个大城市，对不对？

5. 在李友的老家一年四季可以做哪些事？

6. 王德中去过李友家吗？你怎么知道？

B. Dialogue II

1. 王朋喜欢美国的生活吗？

2. 小林去过北京吗？

3. 王朋的老家是个什么样的地方？

4. 北京的气候怎么样？

5. 王朋打算什么时候回北京？

6. 谁说王朋可以当导游？为什么？

Section Two

A. Read the passage and answer the questions (True/False)

> 　　北京是中国的首都，那里春、夏、秋、冬气候不一样。北京夏天很热，有的时候很闷，是最不舒服的季节。冬天很冷，但是很好玩，可以到滑冰场去滑冰。春天的北京非常漂亮，公园里，马路旁，到处开满了花，但是因为风很大，没有秋天舒服。秋天是北京游客最多的季节，最漂亮的地方是北京西边的香山，每年一到看红叶的时候，香山上到处都是人。

( ) 1. 北京的气候四季分明。
( ) 2. 北京的冬天又冷又不好玩，是最不舒服的季节。
( ) 3. 北京的春天游客最多。
( ) 4. 北京的春天比秋天舒服。
( ) 5. 秋天的时候，香山的游客很多。

B. Read the passage and answer the questions (True/False)

> 　　白老师的老家在高雄，高雄是台湾的第二大城市，也是一个海港，有一百多万人口。高雄的气候一年四季变化不太大，春天、冬天凉快一点，从来不下雪。夏天很热，下午常常下大雨，有的时候还有台风。秋天的天气跟夏天差不多。白老师有个姐姐住在波士顿附近的一个小镇，他们已经十多年没见面了。白老师的姐姐告诉他，美国东部秋天的红叶非常漂亮，但是可以看红叶的时间很短，只有两个星期。白老师打算今年十月中到波士顿去玩半个月，他的姐姐会带他到各地去看红叶。

（　）1. 白老师的老家是一个有一百多万人口的海港。

（　）2. 高雄的气候每个季节都很不一样。

（　）3. 高雄夏天的时候会下大雨，也会有飓风。

（　）4. 高雄的秋天比夏天凉快得多。

（　）5. 白老师跟他的姐姐已经很久没见面了。

（　）6. 白老师的姐姐住在美国东部的一个大城市里。

（　）7. 白老师想在波士顿住两个星期。

C. This is a map of Taiwan. Underline all the Chinese characters that you can recognize and also circle the names of the cities that you have learned.

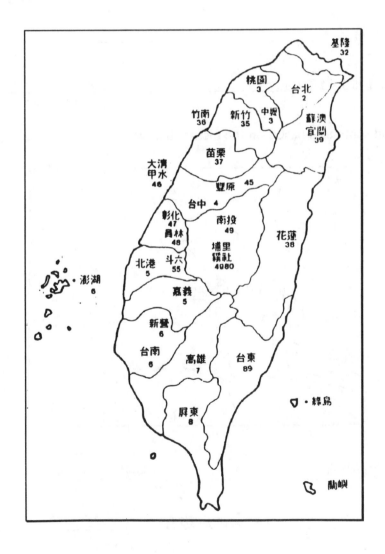

IV. Writing and Grammar Exercises

Section One

A. Following the model, complete the sentences using "以为..."

Example:今天星期五，===>今天星期五，我以为是星期四呢。

1. 学中文不太难，_____。

2. 他没有健康保险，_____。

3. 你怎么现在才来，_____。

4. 他篮球打得非常好，_____。

5. 你昨天去公园玩了吗？_____。

B. Complete the sentences based on the picture below.

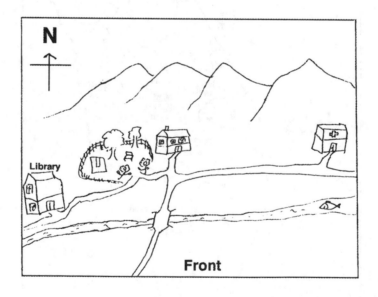

我宿舍的前面有_____，东边是_____，

西边是_____。宿舍的后边有_____。

宿舍和图书馆中间是_____。

C. Following the model, rewrite the sentences below.

Example: 台北的夏天很热, 东京的夏天也很热。

===> 台北的夏天跟东京差不多, 都很热。

1. 打篮球很有意思, 打网球也很有意思。

2. 这件红衣服很好看, 那件白衣服也不难看。

3. 从宿舍到图书馆很近, 到电脑中心也不远。

4. 这家中国饭馆很便宜, 那家韩国饭馆也不贵。

5. 从洛杉矶到台北, 华航的机票是$1, 500, 西北航空公司的机票是$1, 499, 都很贵。

D. Complete the sentences based on the picture on next page.

我房间的墙上挂_____。

床的旁边放 _____。

书桌的左边 _____ 衣柜。

衣柜 _____衣服。

E. Give the Chinese equivalents to the following terms for relatives.

1. grandpa & grandma (on father's side) :

2. grandpa & grandma (on mother's side) :

3. mom's brother and his wife:

4. elder brother's wife :

5. younger sister's husband:

6. granddaughter (on daughter's side) :

F. Complete the following sentences with 比方说.

1. 我的家乡一年四季都很好，_____。

2. 他的亲戚很多，_____。

3. 我春假有很多计划，_____。

4. 加州什么都有，_____。

5. 麻州的风景很好，_____。

G. Answer the following questions using adj./V + 是 + adj./V, 可是/ 但是.

Example: *A:* 那件衬衫好看吗？

B: 那件衬衫好看是好看，可是太贵了。

1. *A:* 日本饭好吃吗？
   B:

2. *A:* 滑雪有意思吗？
   B:

3. *A:* 你喜欢打篮球吗？
   B:

4. *A:* 你租的公寓便宜吗？
   B:

H. Translate the following into Chinese.

1. I thought he was dead. (以为)

2. Behind the store is the computer center. (existence)

3. Your hometown doesn't sound bad at all. (听起来)

4. I can write almost all the characters from Lesson One to Lesson Ten.
    (topic-comment, 差不多)

5. There is a very good restaurant across the street from the university.

6. I plan to go to the mountains to ski during the spring break.

7. Li You has been to many places such as Massachusetts, California, Beijing, and so on.
    (比方说)

8. She likes to read with the TV on. (开着)

9. I don't like to eat while standing up.

10. She lives in the countryside. There is a river near her house. Many trees were planted along the river. In spring, the flowers bloom abundantly in the trees. (着)

11. The beef in that restaurant is delicious, but very expensive. (Adj./V 是 Adj./V)

12. I thought that your aunt was a tour guide.

13. He wrote his name on my dictionary.

14. My uncle is working in San Francisco.

15. It sounds like California's scenery is extremely beautiful.

Section Two

A. Write a paragraph to describe the environment and climate of your hometown.

B. Write a paragraph to introduce your family members, including what they do and where they live.

Lesson Twenty-Three   At the Airport

I. Listening Comprehension

Section One (Listen to the tape for the textbook)

A. Dialogue I (True/False)

(   ) 1.   Li You helped Wang Peng pack.
(   ) 2.   Wang Peng drove to the airport by himself.
(   ) 3.   The airport parking lot was completely full.
(   ) 4.   The man's luggage was overweight.
(   ) 5.   The man has no carry-on luggage.
(   ) 6.   The woman cried because she did not want to leave her parents.
(   ) 7.   The man will be back after a month.
(   ) 8.   The woman asked the man to call her.
(   ) 9.   The man promised the woman that he will drive carefully.
(   ) 10.   The woman wished the man a nice trip.

B. Dialogue II (True/False)

(   ) 1.   Wang Peng's cousin came to the airport to meet him because Wang Peng's parents could not come.
(   ) 2.   Wang Peng's cousin is younger than him.
(   ) 3.   Wang Peng has lost some weight.
(   ) 4.   Wang Peng was on the airplane for more than 20 hours.
(   ) 5.   Wang Peng's grandparents passed away a few years ago.
(   ) 6.   They will go home in Wang Peng's cousin's car.

Section Two (Listen to the tape for the workbook)

A. Narrative (Multiple choice)

(   ) 1.   How many years has Little Gao's aunt lived in Los Angeles?
     a. More than ten years.
     b. Almost ten years.
     c. Twenty years.
     d. Ten months.

(   ) 2.   Where did she and her friends have dinner yesterday afternoon?
     a. At a restaurant in Boston.
     b. At one of her friends' house.
     c. At a Chinese restaurant in Los Angeles.
     d. At her own house.

(   ) 3.   Her furniture was _____ last week.
     a. sold   b. shipped
     c. given to friends   d. rented out

129

(   ) 4. Today she is taking _____ to the airport.
    a. three suitcases full of clothes
    b. three suitcases and some gifts
    c. three suitcases of gifts from her friends in Los Angeles
    d. three suitcases of gifts for her friends in Boston

(   ) 5. At the airport, Little Gao's aunt _____.
    a. bid farewell to her friends repeatedly
    b. talked for a long time to her friends but forgot to say good bye
    c. was too emotional to say anything
    d. wanted to remain silent because she spoke too much yesterday

(   ) 6. Which of the following statements best reflects Little Gao's aunt's feelings as she
      prepares to leave?
    a. Little Gao's aunt realizes that Los Angeles is a much better city than she
       thought.
    b. Little Gao's aunt feels it is very hard to leave her friends.
    c. Little Gao's aunt realizes that she will miss the Chinese restaurants in
       Los Angeles.
    d. Little Gao's aunt feels very sad to be travelling alone.

B. Dialogue (Multiple choice)
(   ) 1. The dialogue is most likely to have taken place _____.
      a. at the Chicago airport
      b. on the airplane
      c. at the Boston airport
      d. at the Los Angeles airport

(   ) 2. Approximately how many hours did the trip take altogether?
    a. three   b. four and half   c. six   d. seven

(   ) 3. What was the weather probably like when the dialogue was taking place?
      It was _____.
      a. sunny but cold
      b. cold and rainy
      c. snowy
      d. windy and rainy

(   ) 4. How did the woman feel on her arrival? She felt _____.
      a. cold but not hungry
      b. both cold and hungry
      c. neither cold nor hungry
      d. hungry but not cold

II. Speaking Exercises

Section One (Answer the questions in Chinese based on the dialogues)

A. Dialogue I

1. What does Wang Peng intend to do during the summer vacation?
2. What did Li You remind Wang Peng to do when Wang Peng was about to go on a journey?
3. Did they find a parking space at the airport? Please explain.
4. What did the woman ask the man? How did the man reply?
5. What did the woman say to the man after checking in his luggage?
6. What did the man say to the woman when he found out why she was crying?
7. What did the man promise the woman to do after returning to his country?
8. What did the woman ask the man to do?
9. What did the man say to the woman before he boarded the plane?
10. What did the woman say to the man before he boarded the plane?

B. Dialogue II
1. What did Wang Peng's cousin say to him when he saw Wang Peng? How did Wang Peng reply?
2. What did the woman say to Wang Peng? How did Wang Peng reply?
3. How did Wang Peng reply when the woman said that Wang Peng must be awfully tired?
4. Who is waiting for them at home? Why?

Section Two

A. The semester is over now; you are in the airport seeing your best friend off. Your friend is kind of sad. You promise that you will call him/her. He/she hopes that you can visit him/her when you have time.

B. Find one or two classmates to role play the following situation. You just got off the airplane. Your family members have come to meet you at the airport. It has been two years since you last saw your family. You want to know how everybody is doing. They want to know if you are tired from the long trip and what your life abroad was like.

C. How do you say "Have a nice trip!" in Chinese?

D. How do you say "Take care of yourself." in Chinese?

III. Reading Exercises

Section One

A. Dialogue I

1. 王朋为什么要回中国？

2. 他是怎么到机场的？

3. 为什么李友花了很久时间才找到一个停车位？

4. 王朋坐哪家航空公司的飞机？

5. 王朋有几件行李要托运？

6. 上飞机的时候要什么东西？

7. 王朋在什么地方上飞机？

8. 王朋和李友现在在机场的什么地方？

9. 你想李友为什么哭了？

10. 李友要王朋打电话给她吗？为什么？

11. 送人的时候，可以说什么客气的话？

B. Dialogue II

1. 哪些人到机场来接王朋？

2. 谁要帮王朋拿行李？

3. 为什么王朋瘦了五公斤？

4. 王朋坐了多长时间的飞机才到北京？

5. 王朋家里还有哪些人？

6. 王朋的父母开车来接王朋吗？你是怎么知道的？

Section Two

A. Read the passage and answer the questions. (True/False)

小张第一次来美国读书的时候，他的爸爸、妈妈和妹妹都到机场去送他。因为小张的行李太多了，他们家的汽车放不下，所以爸爸跟妈妈开家里的车，小张跟妹妹是坐出租汽车到机场去的。因为这是小张第一次出国，他的爸妈都很担心，一直跟他说到美国以后应该注意的事。要上飞机的时候，小张的妈妈流了眼泪，妹妹也哭了。小张的爸爸要小张一到美国就打电话回家，告诉他们他到美国了。

( ) 1. 小张出国的时候，他的父母和妹妹都到机场去送他。

( ) 2. 小张跟妹妹开车去机场。

( ) 3. 小张来美国以前没有出过国。

( ) 4. 小张来美国读书，他的父母一点都不担心。

( ) 5. 小张要上飞机的时候，他的妈妈、妹妹都哭了。

B. Read the passage and answer the questions. (True/False)

今天小白的父母和哥哥到高雄机场去接她。小白到美国念了两年书，现在她从研究所毕业了。小白一直没有回过家，所以家里的人都很想念她。飞机应该晚上十点三刻到高雄机场，可是在台北转机的时候，因为天气不好，飞机晚了一个半小时。飞机到了以后，小白又等了差不多半个多小时才等到她托运的两件行李。虽然小白的爸爸妈妈等了两个多小时，有点累了，可是他们一看到了小白就一点都不觉得累了。

( ) 1. 小白是在美国读研究所的。

( ) 2. 小白等到研究所毕业以后才回台湾。

( ) 3. 小白的飞机从美国直飞高雄。

( ) 4. 小白的行李都是自己随身带着，没有托运。

( ) 5. 小白见到她的家人的时候应该差不多半夜一点钟了。

IV. Writing and Grammar Exercises
Section One

A. Complete the following short conversations with 就行了.

1. *A:* 我下个月就要去中国了，你有什么事情吗？(写信)

   B: _____ 。

2. 学生：明天的考试，我们应该怎么复习？(最后三课)

   老师：_____ 。

3. *A:* 到学校图书馆怎么走？(往右拐，一直往前走)

   B: _____ 。

4. *A:* 我最近越来越瘦了，怎么办？(多吃饭)

   B: _____ 。

5. *A:* 我住的房间很舒服，可是太贵。我不知道怎么办。(找朋友一起住)

   B: _____ 。

B. Fill in the blanks with "才"、"还"

   我的妹妹很小，上个月_____两岁。这个月我回家的时候见到她，没想到_____过了一个月她已经会说很多话了。她不但会说几句英文，_____会说一点中文，而且她的发音_____不错。

C. Complete the following sentences using "好像".

1. 他一直流眼泪，也不说话，_____。
   (sad)

2. 他家里的书多极了，_____。
   (library)

3. 他开车开得很好，_____。
   (drive for a long time)

4. 回到房间以后她一直不说话，_____。
   (unhappy)

5. 他见了我不说话，_____。
   (do not know me)

D. Fill in the blanks using "的，得 or 地"

　　我_____朋友去中国已经一年了。昨天他回来了。我高兴_____去飞机场接他。一年没见，他好像长_____更高了。他送给我_____礼物是一本中文书，可是我_____中文学_____不太好，所以看不懂。因为我们很久没在一起了，所以昨天晚上我们去一家很贵_____饭馆好好_____庆祝了一下。

E. Translate the following into Chinese.

1. The parking lot is filled with cars. We almost failed to find a parking space. (差一点)

2. I will write to you as soon as I get to New York. Take good care of yourself. (多保重)

3. I don't want to buy another computer. This one will do just fine. (就行了)

4. My mother used to say, "Don't talk while you eat. It's a bad habit." (一边...一边)

5. After I learned who it was, I almost let out a cry. (...以后，差一点)

6. He seems as though he doesn't want to go to the opera with Li You. (好像)

7. The food in this Japanese restaurant is not bad. (还)

8. Wang Peng is only two years older than Li You. (才)

9. Grandmother (maternal) doesn't have the strength to carry her luggage. Hurry up and help her carry the luggage. (V + potential complement)

10. My brother's desk is very small. (的, 地, 得)

11. He walks very fast but runs pretty slow. (的, 地, 得)

12. After eating her lunch quickly, she went to her class. (的, 地, 得)

13. I was not accustomed to eating American food, so I lost 10 kilograms. (V + potential complement)

14. The airplane is about to take off! Please take good care of yourself. Bon voyage.

Section Two

A. Write a letter to your friends in Chinese. Tell them that you are going to China to see them, ask them to pick you up at the airport, and give them your flight information.

B. Write a paragraph describing your experience of flying. Be sure to mention the food and the seat.